WHAT PEOPLE ARE SAYING ABOUT
SANDBOX WISDOM

"*Sandbox Wisdom* is a true gem. Tom does a remarkable job at making the importance of human connections being really what it's all about. Just when you think you know it all, read *Sandbox Wisdom*, and then read it again. An insightful and refreshing book sure to be a <u>top</u> seller."

—Donald E. Graham
    Chief Executive Officer, The Washington Post

"In *Sandbox Wisdom*, Tom Asacker puts us back in touch with our instincts on how to communicate to customers and employees, and gives us "ah ha" moments on how to brand and market."

—Ivan Seidenberg
    Chairman and CEO, Bell Atlantic

"This is not another formulaic business book written with perfect hindsight about some increasingly irrelevant business model. The lessons here are fast, timeless and under your nose."

—Scott Bedbury
    CEO, BrandStream, Author of *A Brand New World*

"Absolutely excellent! Business leaders should grab a shovel and a pail and climb into this sandbox of wisdom. They'll be amazed at the treasures they'll uncover there."

—David Schottelkotte
    Manager, Employee Communications, Procter & Gamble

"*Sandbox Wisdom* is a refreshing reminder that many of the lessons learned early in one's life should never be forgotten."

—Jeff Shuman
    Professor and Director of Entrepreneurial Studies at
    Bentley College, Author of *The Rhythm of Business*

"*Sandbox Wisdom* is illuminating. It's about seeing past all of the debris of adulthood to the simple yet powerful truths of our inner child."

—Bill Glasser

Innovation Manager, Environmental Protection Agency

"Tom's content and style re-ignites a much needed spark of purpose, passion, and playfulness into the workplace."

—Deb Titus

Managing Partner, Human Capital Solutions, LLC

"How refreshing! The message of *Sandbox Wisdom*, that we need to simplify our business and brand building efforts, is incredibly timely. Flying in the face of the latest models and technology, Tom Asacker reminds us that ultimately, business is about the human element."

—Jennie Bettles

Founder and CEO, GlobalVue

"Tom Asacker always brings a fresh perspective to marketing and business. His *Sandbox Wisdom* offers wisdom from Dr. Seuss to Gandhi and practical advice from his many years of creating emotional connections between businesses and their customers."

—Joyce Wycoff

Founder Innovation Network, Author of *Mindmapping*

"Tom Asacker provides a game plan to translate the lessons of the sandbox to the boardroom, while simultaneously revitalizing our personal and professional lives."

—Phil Fragasso

Managing Director, Liberty Funds

"*Sandbox Wisdom* reminds us that what we learn after we know it all is what really counts."

—John Koulopoulos

Senior VP - Investments, A. G. Edwards & Sons, Inc.

"A wonderful story that will certainly cause me to look within myself for the answers!"

—Jim Ricciardelli

Director, Ecommerce Channels, Lycos, Inc.

SANDBOX WISDOM

REVOLUTIONIZE YOUR BRAND
WITH THE GENIUS OF CHILDHOOD

TOM ASACKER

Eastside Publishing

This book is printed on acid-free paper.

Published by:

EASTSIDE
Eastside Publishing

P.O. Box 368
Manchester, New Hampshire 03105

ISBN: 0-9677528-0-9

Manufactured in the United States of America
March 2000
10 9 8 7 6 5 4 3 2 1
First Edition

This book is available at substantial discounts for bulk purchases.
For information, mail to Eastside Publishing or visit our home page at
www.sandboxwisdom.com.

To my father, for always giving me the two things I needed most—trust and love. And to my two Angels, Alexandra and Andrea, who will always have mine.

INTRODUCTION

You have brains in your head, and feet in your shoes.
You can steer yourself in any direction you choose.

- Dr. Seuss

✳

*W*hat's your brand? Is it your company? Your product? Your store? Your department? You? My dream—the dream that *you* have the power to make come true—is that this little book will help you separate the "truth"—about branding, marketing, selling, and corporate culture—from the "facts": all of those trendy and complicated techniques, theories, and concepts being promoted as magic potions for growth. And then—once you've rediscovered the "truth"—you will go out, challenge the status quo, and *really* change things. You'll liberate your unique inner voice and inspire, innovate, and make profound improvements in yourself, your business, and in people's lives. You'll create a brand truly worthy of remark.

Sandbox Wisdom is a way for you to reconnect to those simple, yet powerful human "truths" that you once knew instinctively, but may have long since forgotten. It's a way to awaken the subconscious wisdom of your childhood and revitalize your business, and your life. Starting right now, stop waiting for others to lead and inspire you. Instead, do as Gandhi recommended and be the change that you want to see in others. After all, you do have brains in your head and feet in your shoes. You *can* steer yourself in any direction you choose.

CHAPTER ONE

*children guessed (but only a few) and
down they forgot as up they grew . . .*

- e. e. cummings

✳

*S*preadsheets don't lie. The words repeated themselves in the CEO's head like a mantra. *Spreadsheets don't lie.*

"Bill? Bill? . . . You need anything? I'm leaving now."

The CEO looked up from his desk, a pile of spreadsheets and printouts covering every square inch of mahogany wood.

"Huh? No thanks. Go on home."

His assistant nodded. "You should too, you know. You look exhausted."

"I'll be heading out soon."

After his assistant shut the door, Bill again returned to his spreadsheets. He couldn't understand it. He had tried everything to push the company's performance back up to where it should be. He had hired consultants, sent key people to motivational conferences, invested heavily in technology and education, met with every department head as well as most of the employees. He had never spent so many exhausting hours at work. His wife said he'd become "a shadow husband."

I am in the shadows, he thought. *Trying to make this company work again . . . and more in the dark than ever before.*

The spreadsheets told of a corporation with sagging profits. Morale was at an all-time low—his own as well as his employees'. *Spreadsheets don't lie. What we're doing isn't working. So much for expensive consultants.*

Bill's phone rang. He looked at his Rolex. The irony wasn't lost on him. *I have all the trappings of success. Right down to my watch. But I can't make my company tick.* "Six-thirty? Where the heck did the day go?"

He picked up the receiver.

"Bill West."

"Bill, it's Jim."

He instantly recognized the voice of his old college roommate. "Jim? How are you? I haven't spoken to you since . . . when? Last Christmas?"

"I'm doing great. I just got back from a vacation with Susan. We went to a Costa Rican rain forest. Unbelievable trip. Before that, very busy. We're experiencing unprecedented growth. I am so jazzed about what's going on."

"That's great," Bill said, while his insides churned. The industry buzzed with talk of how his old friend had turned around sales in his division.

"How've you been, Bill?"

"The truth or the whitewashed version?"

"Between old friends? Truth, of course."

"Lousy. We're in a big-time slump. *I'm* in a big-time slump. I'm trying everything, but nothing's working."

"Well, I'm in town and I know it's kind of late notice, but do you want to meet for dinner?"

"Sure. Where are you staying?"

✳

Within an hour, the two old friends were having a drink at a dark-wood-paneled steakhouse in the city.

"I don't want to monopolize the conversation, Jim. I do want to hear all about your trip and Susan and the kids. But I am just at my wit's end. What the hell is going on here? Why aren't any of my methods working?"

"Maybe you're trying too hard."

"Nonsense, Jim. You and I have worked harder than anyone I know. But did it ever seem like work?"

"Not really."

"Yeah . . . sure there are times you feel frustrated, but it used to be enough to just get up in the morning. The adrenaline rush. You still have that. You came back from vacation energized. Pumped. And me? I can't see past the numbers. I can't see past the mess."

"Maybe you've hired too many consultants. Everyone has an opinion, but what's in your gut?"

"An ulcer."

The two men laughed as a waiter brought them thick slabs of prime rib.

"Listen," Jim said as he cut into his dinner, "can you stand one more opinion?"

"Sure."

"I think you need to see my guru."

"Guru? *You* went to see a guru?"

"Not a meditation guru, Bill. A business guru. At least

that's what he is to me. And not just anyone. The best. Two years ago, I was where you are."

"I do remember now . . . sales were stagnant and profits were non-existent. But you totally turned that around."

"With a little help."

"Your guru?"

"Trust me, Bill?"

"Implicitly."

"Let me make a few phone calls tomorrow. I'm sure the guru will fit you in. Challenging cases intrigue him."

"I'll be ready. You just name the time and place."

That Thursday afternoon, Bill found himself driving to a gas station on the edge of town. Jim's instructions had been vague. Bill was supposed to be at the station by 1:15. He would leave his car there and the guru, a man named Richard Falcon, would meet him and drive them to their next destination.

"Everybody simply calls this guy Falcon. You know how some people fit their name?" Jim had said. "Well, this guy's got piercing vision."

Bill had stared at the directions as he took them down over the phone.

"Why can't I just meet him at our actual destination?"

"Listen Bill. It's how Falcon works. You gotta trust me."

"You're not sending me on some Outward Bound thing are you Jim? I'm not going to end up in some swamp with a compass and a Swiss Army knife and one day's supply of rations, am I?

"Just trust me."

As Bill drove that Thursday to the appointed station, he mused; *I better not be going on some wild goose chase. I'm wearing my best Armani suit.*

He pulled his Lexus into the charming little service station. It had a quaint sign right out of the 1950s, and the adjoining mechanic's garage was painted crisp white. At the old-fashioned pump, stood the station's lone customer—a big man in an expensive suit leaning his elbow on a cherry-red Porsche. He was talking to a slim, silver-haired mechanic in blue overalls. At the sight of the man's tailored suit, Bill relaxed. *At least no wilderness adventure. This guy will know what I'm dealing with.*

He pulled into a parking spot, strode across the concrete to the big man, and extended his hand.

"It's a pleasure to meet you. I'm Bill West. Thank you so much for meeting me on such short notice."

The man raised his eyebrow and returned the firm handshake Bill proffered.

"Nice to meet you, Bill. By any chance are you looking for Falcon?"

Bill nodded.

"Well, then you need to meet this gentleman here," he gestured to the mechanic.

Bill tried to keep a startled expression off his face as he turned to the mechanic.

"Mr. Falcon, I'm Bill West. I'm sorry . . . I just assumed . . ."

"A pleasure to meet you," Falcon broke in, a bemused twinkle in his eye. "Come on, we have to hurry if we're going to make our next appointment."

Settled into a classic Barracuda, the two men headed down the highway.

"I brought all my spreadsheets, the performance charts from the last four quarters. Any fact or figure you need, I've got right here," Bill pointed at the briefcase he'd brought.

"Actually, we don't need them. We're on our way to meet our teacher."

"Great. Between the three of us, I sure hope we can get this company back on track. I wonder all the time . . . is it the marketing? The advertising? My sales team? What is it?"

"Trust me, this teacher will give you clarity that you've never had before. She helped me."

"She? Okay. Great. Was your garage not doing well?"

Falcon roared with laughter. When he finally stopped laughing, he smiled and spoke, "I used to head a multi-million dollar company that I built from the ground floor up. And that was in the *pre*-Internet days when profits mattered."

Bill stared at his new acquaintance, impressed.

"I wanted to take it public and then retire so I could pursue my hobby of restoring classic cars. The only problem was I felt completely stagnant. After a lifetime in business, I just couldn't get excited about it anymore. I lost my passion. And then I met our teacher. And everything changed forever."

The two men talked about companies and cars, and about fifteen minutes later, Falcon pulled the Barracuda up in front of an elementary school.

This guy has got to be kidding me. Our teacher is an actual teacher? Some kindergarten expert is going to teach me about marketing and profit margins? What the heck was Jim thinking when he set this up? And now I'm stuck. I don't even have a car to make a graceful exit.

Falcon turned off the engine and looked at Bill with total compassion.

"Lesson number one, Bill. Keep an open mind. I know your brain is rattling through a thousand reasons why I'm a crackpot. I'm wearing overalls. My fingernails are dirty. And I've just taken you to a schoolyard. When you pulled into my station, did you guess I was a former CEO? Worth millions? I say that not to impress you, but to impress upon you that assumptions get you nowhere in life. They close doors, not open them. Come on . . . here's our teacher."

As Falcon said this, jubilant children streamed out of opened doors. A little girl ran towards Falcon, two long, black braids streaming behind her. She was missing her two front teeth—immediately evident in her grin.

"Grandpa!" She threw her arms around Falcon's neck as he knelt to greet her. Cheeks flushed, she was the epitome of childish glee.

"Annie, I'd like you to meet Mr. West."

Bill knelt down and reached out a gentle hand, "It's very nice to meet you Annie."

"Nice to meet you too, Mr. West," Annie smiled, shaking his hand. "Do you have any kids?"

"No. Not yet. Maybe someday. I really like children."

"Good. Because I like most grownups. Not scary ones like the lunch lady who never smiles. But nice ones. And if you know Grandpa, you must be as nice as he is."

She removed her brightly-colored backpack and climbed into the back seat of the car, as Falcon opened the door. Bill looked at Falcon expectantly.

"Are we waiting for her teacher?"

"Her teacher? Oh . . . no. Annie *is* the teacher."

"What?"

"No assumptions, remember? And actually, she's not really our teacher. She's simply our assistant. Your experience with her is your teacher. See . . . only experiences have value. You experience something, you live through it, you know it."

"Yeah, but . . ."

"Listen, Bill. What holds people back from experiencing new things? Why do they limit their experiences? Because they perceive risks. Today, with me and Annie here, there are no risks. There are no customers, no shareholders, no media people—just you and me and one adorable little girl who's ready for her ice cream cone. What do you have to lose?"

"Nothing, I guess," Bill said as he slid into the front seat.

If nothing else, I can have a good laugh about this someday. But he had to admit one thing, Falcon had an air of serenity and real happiness about him.

Hope it's contagious.

CHAPTER TWO

*We want people to feel with us
more than to act for us.*

-George Eliot

❋

"*D*idn't you just pass a couple of Dairy Barns on this stretch of highway?" Bill asked Falcon as they continued driving.

"We never go there," Annie piped up from the back seat.

"Why not?"

"It's just not as good as Udder Delight."

"Never been there."

"It's delicious! And fun."

"Really? So what's your favorite flavor, Annie?"

"Peppermint stick. But I always get a taste of something else, just in case I think I might like it better. Mr. Garcia gives out little tastes in these little tiny cups—as many tastes as you want."

"And this guy's rum raisin is udderly delightful," Falcon joked.

Well, I sure hope this ice cream is worth the drive, Bill thought to himself as they passed yet another sit-down ice cream parlor along the way. He looked in the back seat and noticed that Annie was engrossed in a book. He turned to Falcon.

"She's adorable."

"I think so, too. I also notice she seems to have no problem turning the pages. I want to thank you for that."

"What? Thank me for what?"

"Oh . . . just a joke. But I noticed when I introduced the two of you at the schoolyard that you knelt down and shook her hand very softly. You didn't give her one of those vise-like handshakes."

"Come on . . . like I'm going to crush your granddaughter's hand," Bill smiled.

"Of course not, I guess. But you also really looked her in the eye."

"I like kids."

"Well, we're almost at Udder Delight. But I'll give you something to think about as you ponder what flavor you want."

"What's that?" Bill asked, eager to get on with the business aspect of their afternoon together.

"Why did you shake Annie's hand so gently?"

"Because she's a little girl."

"But I shook your hand at the station, and you had a strong grip."

"It wouldn't be appropriate to shake her hand like that."

"Ah-ha. . . . . you, my friend, have just had an Ah-ha moment. Do you realize it?"

"Sorry Falcon. Now I'm really lost."

"You said it wouldn't be *appropriate* to shake her hand with a vise grip. What I want to know is this: If, in business, you meet someone who has a gentle handshake, what do you do?"

"I give them my usual handshake. I was taught in business school—like everyone else for that matter—that the first greeting you offer in a business situation is a firm handshake. Leaves a strong impression."

"Uh-huh. Well, I think it's time to bury those B-school myths. That kind of handshake is all about showing off your power and strength. And Bill . . . people don't deal with you because they're impressed with you. They do it because they *feel* like it. Because they trust you. Your base of power—if you wish to think of it that way—is feelings. The emotional bond. And do you know who people trust—and bond with— the most?"

Bill looked down and to the left, obviously searching for the right answer.

"Think about children, Bill."

"Other children?"

"Exactly. They trust people like themselves. People with the same characteristics. So if someone has a soft handshake, give that person a soft one back. Acknowledge that you understand and respect that person. You want them to feel comfortable with you. You must respect how others shake hands . . . how they speak . . . how they do business. Because business is about connections, being comfortable and feeling safe with the person you choose to do business with. All this power stuff is old news. The way things used to be. Time for a change."

Bill nodded. "An Ah-ha moment."

"Precisely. A paradigm shift. A change in the way you think about the world. Because when you change your mind, Bill, *then* you change your life."

At that, Falcon pulled his Barracuda into the parking lot of a picturesque ice cream parlor that resembled a barn. A college-age young woman in overalls with a red bandanna around her neck was greeting people as they emerged from the cars or strolled up to the doors.

"Welcome again to Udder Delight, Mr. Falcon. Hi Annie!" The young woman knelt down and pulled a bright-colored sticker off a roll. "How about a kitten sticker today for my number-one kitten fan?"

Annie beamed, "Thanks, Marci."

"That's a beautiful tie, Sir. Would you like to put a sticker on it?" The young woman joked with Bill.

"Thank you, but I think I'll pass. I'm just here for the ice cream."

With that, Falcon, Bill, and Annie entered Udder Delight.

The owner, Mr. Garcia, greeted them with a wide smile. "Mr. Falcon. Welcome. Rum raisin today? Peppermint stick for the lady?"

"Rum raisin for me, Albert. But Annie might want to try something else. And Bill? Something for you?"

"I'll take a scoop of . . . hmm . . . I'll take a scoop of mint chocolate chip."

"Coming right up. I'll send it over to your usual booth. And in the meantime, I'll help Annie here to some first-class taste-testing."

Mr. Garcia turned all his attention to Annie. The parlor was fairly empty, with just two or three tables of people. Annie moved along the glass-enclosed freezer case, standing on tiptoe and peering in at the homemade ice cream Udder Delight was known for. Like a child excited by the magic of a Christmas store display, she oohed and ahhed and took her time pointing out flavors and tasting each one very carefully.

Bill and Falcon sat at their booth and drank the ice water that had been brought out to them by a waiter in farmer's overalls.

"Cute place."

"Yeah. And wait'll you see how busy it gets when school lets out. You know, Bill, before all the commotion, I want to ask you another question. When you acknowledged my little Annie there at the schoolyard, you knelt down. You ever do that with a customer?"

"Get down on my knees? Sure, when I'm begging to close that big sale."

Falcon laughed, "No, I mean deal with them on their level."

"I don't know. I think I do."

"Really? On their level? Whatever that level is? Because when you say hello to someone, you're not just exchanging a bit of social pleasantry. You're doing a hell of a lot more. You're saying 'trust me.' Because, nowadays, people are extremely skeptical. They can smell a sales pitch or a phony from a mile off."

"Of course. I *must* deal with people on their level. I know that I can't stand it when someone gets past my assistant, and the call is just a cold call. Or being cornered by a phony at a meeting or a cocktail party."

"Sure. But go another level deeper. *Why* do you dislike it so intensely?"

"I don't know. I guess I feel . . . used. Like this person could care less about my time and doesn't really want to talk to me. They want to talk to my wallet."

"Exactly. Take a minute to think about it. Isn't it the same with marketing and advertising? Most of it is clearly irrelevant; just a bunch of chest-thumping superlatives or lame attempts at humor. So . . . the public perceives that business people are out-of-touch, self-absorbed and motivated by greed, instead of being concerned with the well being of their customers, their employees, their communities. There's no depth to the relationship anymore. We've forgotten—in this technological age—how to slow down, truly empathize and make each contact count as a genuine, sincere encounter. Bill, it's still all about people and their feelings. But we all seem to have forgotten that."

Falcon sighed and looked off into the distance. Then he refocused on Bill, who had taken out a small leather notebook and a Mont Blanc pen.

"I hear you, Falcon. I've forgotten some of this myself. I want to write all this down so I don't forget it again."

"Okay, but remember, today is about our experience. So it's more important that you take notice than to take notes. Got it?"

"I understand. And I hear you about customers' feelings. I know I get busy and forget that. I just don't have the time the way I used to."

"Can't let that happen. You're in the feelings business, Bill. Everyone is. You need to focus on the experience your customers—and your employees—have with you and your company. Respect, authenticity, empathy, being vulnerable."

Falcon paused, then continued. "Hey . . . here's a good example, I think. Do you ever recall someone getting down to your level when you were younger? Say, in college or right after? Maybe a college professor or someone? A person who connected with you even if maybe you weren't as experienced as he or she was?"

"I don't know." Bill paused. "Wait . . . Yes. I remember interviewing for my first job after college. I was twenty-one, and I was one of a handful in my graduating class whose résumé got past the powers that be at a big multinational corporation for its management-training program. I made it through the first two levels of interviews, and I finally met a senior VP in charge of marketing. He had me come into his office. I was nervous as hell. And then . . . he had *me* sit in *his* chair behind *his* desk. Now this wasn't just any chair. It was one of those cushy, butter-soft thousand-dollar leather chairs that swiveled. Any direction I looked, I had a view of the skyline out of his office. Once I was sitting, he pulled a chair up close to me, and we had this heart to heart."

"And how did it make you feel?"

"Incredible. It made a profound difference in my life at

that time. I knew I wanted to be him. Not just sit in his chair, but to be *like* him. To be able to make people feel comfortable like that."

"Honest. Vulnerable. Empathetic. He had all the ingredients of success."

"You know," Bill whispered, "I forgot all about him until now."

"Grandpa!" Annie came running over with her ice cream cone. "Peppermint stick is still my favorite."

"Well . . . there's always next time. Tastes change. But until then, you're still my peppermint stick sweetie."

Annie smiled. "Are you going to call me that when I'm big?"

"Yeah. When you're getting married I'm going to scream out in church, 'There goes the peppermint stick kid!'" Grinning, Falcon grabbed Annie and poked her in the ribs.

Annie collapsed in a fit of laughter. "You always make me laugh, Grandpa."

"I love to make you laugh, Annie. So tell me . . . how was school today?"

Annie's mood changed instantly. "Oh," she sighed. "There's this boy who's been bothering me. He says I'm a baby because I won't go on the highest monkeybar."

Bill West leaned towards Annie, "I know how that can be. Someone picking on you."

"Yeah. But you're big. It's different."

Falcon put his arm around his granddaughter and tugged on her braid. "Did you know I was afraid of spiders when I was a kid?"

Annie's face brightened. "You were?"

"I was. Just like you're afraid of heights. And I never really got over it. Your grandmother is braver about spiders than I am! But that's okay, you know. Everyone's afraid of something."

Annie leaned into his chest, "Thanks. I knew you'd understand. You always make me feel better."

"Here," Falcon fished into his pocket. "Why don't you go play the jukebox." He counted out eight quarters. "This is enough for six songs. Though, Annie, when I was a kid a handful of nickels kept the jukebox going all night long."

Annie departed the table again, clutching her cone and her quarters.

"You are unbelievably good with her," Bill West's voice was admiring.

"Naw. Just real. I don't belittle her fears. And I don't tell her I know how it is unless I really know exactly how it is. But I do try to find common ground. You see, Bill, that's why I said you'd learn a lot from spending the afternoon with Annie as your teacher. If you think like a child, if you become the child, you can learn all the secrets to revitalizing your business sense. You shouldn't manipulate kids—and trust me they spot that from a mile away. You don't pull a power play. You listen. You give them love. You earn their trust. You acknowledge they might be scared, and you share *your* fears—but only if you really do know about fears like theirs. Otherwise, you just acknowledge their feelings, shut up and listen."

"Which is what I'm doing. I'm absorbing everything you say. It makes sense. Trust is the bedrock of every sales relationship. Of any relationship—period."

"Precisely. Trust and being genuine. But what's happened with the advent of technology? We try to make that trust grow in a nanosecond. We don't develop it. Did you watch the owner with Annie? He offered her no less than nine tastes of ice cream. And he never hurried her, even though he knew as well as I that she would choose the peppermint stick in the end. You see . . . kids don't like to be rushed. No one does. And Albert understands that."

"He must just have a knack for understanding kids."

"It's much more than that. Albert is an old friend of mine. He and I have had many talks like the one you and I are having. You know Udder Delight is franchising? And he's not letting any detail change at any of the others. That patience you saw? He feels it's vital to his business." Falcon paused and glanced at the door. "Say Bill . . . what time is it?"

"Three o'clock."

"Oh boy! Watch out. The masses arrive soon. School's out at the high school and junior high."

"Should we leave?"

"No. Let's just observe."

Annie rejoined them and quietly sat eating her ice cream cone and listening to the music of her juke box selections as students streamed in.

18

"This is worse than a 70s disco," Bill remarked. "They're three deep at the counter."

Yet they watched as Albert Garcia and his employees masterfully handled the crowd of students. There was no pushing or annoyance from the crowd as each customer was given a broad smile and a friendly hello. Orders were filled as quickly as possible, but no one seemed to mind a little wait. Amazingly, the proprietor seemed to know most of the students by name, and he doled out praise and encouragement with each scoop.

"Joey, how did that history test go?"

"Great Mr. G. I aced it."

"Second scoop's on me!"

Then he turned to his next customer. "You cut your hair, Amy. I like it. Are you happy with it?"

A shy girl nodded.

"Good. I think the haircut suits you."

Falcon turned to Bill West at the table, "Did you see how that girl's face just lit up when he noticed her hair?"

"Yeah. She's a pretty girl."

"Sure. But she's an adolescent. She doesn't always *feel* that. But he made her feel good. He noticed it. Do you do that with your customers? Notice something that is meaningful to them?"

"No. Seems kind of fake to offer compliments like that."

"Fake? More B-school myth. Our needs, as adults, are not much different from childhood needs. We need to feel complimented, praised, valued. Be genuine when you offer a compliment, and if you *look* for opportunities to praise others it will change your whole outlook on life. I guarantee it."

"It will, huh?" Bill raised a skeptical eyebrow as he polished off the last of his ice cream.

"Sure. Instead of looking for the negative, you'll spend your time looking for the positive. Your outlook—your passion—will change. What is personal charisma, Bill? What is that indefinable something that makes us want to be with someone?"

"Energy?"

"Energy and the fact that they're giving us their pure feelings. Their passion. And if you look for a compliment, if you look for praise, if you look for ways to reward someone's accomplishments—an employee's, a customer's, a supplier's—with words of thanks and real appreciation and admiration on your part, the positive energy you receive back will be a hundredfold. Try it on Annie here. Annie?"

"Yes, Grandpa?"

"Bill here's going to tell you something, and you tell us how it makes you feel."

"Another 'speriment."

"'Speriment?"

"Experiment," Falcon chuckled. "See I believe in what I'm telling you here today with all my heart. When I spend time with Annie, we regard the world as our own big laboratory. We experiment with these concepts all the time. Annie is a—"

"Student of the human menonema!"

"Phenomena?" Bill guessed, with a wry grin.

"Exactly," said Falcon.

Bill looked at the bright-eyed little girl and saw any one of a number of things to compliment—her shiny hair, her toothless smile and how it lit up her face, her enthusiasm.

"Miss Annie," he smiled warmly, "I want to say that I really admire the fact that you're not afraid to try new things. Like the ice cream testing. Has peppermint stick always been your favorite?"

"I used to like cookie dough better."

"Well, you're very inquisitive. And I think that's great!"

"Thank you, Mr. West." She smiled and her nose crinkled up in pleasure. "I liked that."

"When you had to look for something, it was pretty easy, wasn't it?" Falcon asked.

"Yeah. But I get so caught up in things at work. Am I going to remember to stop and notice these things about my customers and my employees?"

"If you don't, I can assure you things won't turn around. These things you get caught up in at work—your in-box and to-do list—are not your job. Your job is people and their feelings. Being focused on others is the key to finding true success. Look at the crowd here. You think the other ice cream places are like this? Albert and his employees never get frustrated. And they attend to all of the little details. The girl with the stickers. The way we didn't have to ask for water, they just brought it right over. The friendliness."

"I can see why the place is popular. And my ice cream was *udderly delightful*."

"I'm telling you . . . the rum raisin is the best. Now, Annie Bananie, where to next?"

"The park. Did you bring the bread?"

"Have two loaves of day-old under the front seat."

Bill looked quizzically at Falcon.

"We're duck people," Annie explained. "We like to feed them at the pond near the park."

"Well, let's go then. And ice cream's on me. This was worth ten thousand ice creams," Bill said as he went to pay.

Mr. Garcia walked over to the register. "Next time you come in," he said, as he opened the drawer, "you can try our chocolate mint chip crunch. You might like it even better than our mint chocolate chip."

"You've been serving a hundred kids here and you still remembered my ice cream flavor?"

"Well, my guess is—since you're spending the day with Mr. Falcon and Annie there—that you now know that business is about feelings and connections. And given the fact that people today have a seemingly unlimited number of options—think of how many ice cream franchises there are and how many ice cream stores are in this town alone—it's up to me to be sensitive to my customers' feelings. But here's the trick. I need to anticipate, not just give good customer service. I need to be keenly aware of their emotional needs and provide an engaging experience. More than ever before, it's about people." He looked around. "It's about the children really."

"I'm beginning to see that," Bill replied, as he exited, suddenly sure he would learn more lessons at the duck pond.

BILL'S NOTEPAD

* People respond to genuineness. Make sure we don't lose sight of this.

* Make sure our company is a safe place for people to express vulnerabilities. That way we won't be afraid to show that to our customers.

* We respond to others who are like us. Next company meeting, tell the story about the handshake-thing that Falcon told me. They'll all relate, I think.

* It's about feelings. We're in the feelings business. Get everyone in the company to say this over and over 'til they mean it.

* Provide a pleasing experience—not just good customer service.

CHAPTER THREE

You can observe a lot by watching.

- Yogi Berra

✳

"Ff you had told me a week ago that I would find a trip to an ice cream store 'enlightening,' I would have called you crazy."

"Visionaries risk being misunderstood, Bill. What we must remember is we are trying to change the world."

"The world? I'd settle for a solid quarter of profits and happy stockholders."

"If we change minds one at a time, we *will* change the world. The world is not a static thing. We're part of it. We can change it. You simply have to be willing to risk being vulnerable and open."

Bill glanced in the back seat at Annie, contentedly looking out her window, as crowded suburbs became more pastoral.

"It's easy to be vulnerable with sweet kids like Annie. But what about the sharks in the corporate waters?"

"The Greeks told us that what makes heroes interesting is not simply their great strengths but also their weaknesses. I've learned more from my granddaughter than from all the great books I've read or courses I've taken or deals I've sealed. The wisdom of children is their inability to conceal their feelings. When Annie wants to be loved, she doesn't pout or play games. She simply snuggles against me and puts her head on my chest. In children, that type of honesty and vulnerability isn't perceived as weakness."

Falcon made a left-hand turn into a beautiful park and drove toward the duck pond. Couples strolled arm in arm, a few teens whizzed by on in-line skates, and children ran under the watchful gazes of their mothers.

"Mr. West," Annie called out from the back seat. "Did you know that if you smile at people they smile back?"

Bill turned his head to look at Annie. "That's because they love that grin of yours. Did the tooth fairy visit?"

She nodded. "I got a dollar. A silver dollar!"

Falcon winked at Bill. "A value-added dollar. Same purchasing power, but a whole lot more pretty to hold."

Annie waved out the window. "Sometimes people even wave back. I sometimes have a contest with my cousin, Frank. We each wave at people out different windows and see who gets the most waves back."

"When our culture stopped waving and saying hello," Falcon said softly, "we lost our connection to others."

Falcon pulled into a parking lot, and they all climbed out of the car and began walking in the general direction of the duck pond. Annie skipped and whistled and waved at passersby.

Bill turned to Falcon. "I've been thinking about our lessons at Udder Delight."

"And?"

"One thing kind of bothers me. What if I don't *feel* like smiling, or waving, or complimenting someone? If I do it anyway, it seems fake. Almost like acting. And the handshake thing . . . if I change my style to match someone else's, I'm not being authentic."

"But we all take on roles when we're dealing with others, Bill. Different situations require us to adopt a different role, even in business. Just because you try on that role doesn't mean that part of you, that role, isn't a 'real' part of you, an authentic part of you. When was the last time you went out for dinner?"

"Last week I took my wife out for dinner. I had been working too many late nights, and then when I was home I was absorbed in work. I decided I needed to take her to Antonio's over on 15th Avenue to just talk. Have an evening of conversation."

"Did you like that place? Would you recommend it to a friend?"

"Sure. Antonio's is a little expensive, but the food is great. My wife had a pasta dish that was cooked to perfection. The service was excellent. Four stars in my book."

"You say the service was excellent. Did you have a waiter or a waitress?"

"Waitress. She was good. Not too obtrusive, but just the right amount of friendliness."

"Do you think she loved being on her feet all night? You think she enjoyed rushing over to the inevitable crabby diner who wanted to send back his food? Racing back and forth to the hot kitchen?"

"Loved it? No." Bill replied. "But it's not her job to love it. She's *supposed* to be friendly. Service with a smile, right?"

"Precisely. It's her *job* to be friendly and smile. There are a thousand waiters and waitresses in town. Her boss wouldn't keep her if she couldn't perform her job amiably. Her job was to make you feel comfortable, to serve your wife and you in a courteous, professional manner. But she put *your* emotional needs ahead of her own. I see that as an act of caring. It doesn't matter if it's her job. You didn't know if she was tired or if she just had a fight with her husband or roommate before she came to work. She slipped into her *role* of professional server. Now do you recall the last time you had lousy service?"

"Do I ever. And let me tell you, the food was good, but the experience was so horrible I'd never go back there. I was at that little French place downtown across from the financial center. This waiter we had was inexcusably rude. He actually sighed *aloud* when someone in our party ordered and then changed her mind. It wasn't like he had put the order into the kitchen. He just had to scratch out what he wrote. And then he just had an attitude all night. We had to ask for everything . . . water refills and condiments. And believe me, I'm pretty easygoing. If he was busy or having an off night and had just smiled once in a while, it would have made all the difference. And it was my wife's best friend's birthday to boot."

"So was he a lousy waiter?"

"Yeah."

"What else?"

"Rude."

"He was also selfish." Falcon added. "He was focused inwardly. He didn't care about you or your feelings. He didn't care that it was a festive night or a special occasion. And his selfishness came through loud and clear. He took away from your experience. It's all about heart. It's asking yourself 'How do I dress to make the other person comfortable? How do I speak? How do I shake hands?' That attention to empathy conveys strength and caring and composure. These qualities attract us and reassure us." Falcon smiled as he watched Annie head toward a flock of geese and ducks. "Just as they did when we were small and helpless."

"Grandpa! Grandpa! Charlie's back!"

"Charlie?" Bill looked around and saw no one else was at the duck pond.

"He's that big white duck there with the soiled feathers. We used to see him all the time. Then he left the pond last winter, and he hasn't been back since. He's Annie's favorite."

Annie took one of the bags of bread from Falcon and approached the flock. Ducks and geese eagerly honked and quacked and grabbed at the bread. Some caught pieces mid-air, a feat that delighted Annie.

"They do tricks!" she squealed.

Other ducks and geese stayed back, satisfied to nibble at the crumbs and cast-offs of the more forward flock members. Charlie was one of them.

"Charlie? What's wrong, Charlie?" Annie approached the duck several times, trying to offer him large hunks of bread, but he backed away nervously.

"Grandpa? What's wrong with Charlie? Last year he was my friend."

"I don't know, Honey. Try standing still. Maybe he just doesn't remember you."

Falcon and Bill moved in closer for a look at the duck.

"He's definitely spooked," Bill said. "And his left wing doesn't rest right across his back."

Falcon motioned Bill back to a large oak tree. Then he whispered, "You know, there was this kid here last year, and I used to catch him throwing rocks at Charlie here. I spoke to that kid several times and even called park services. Who knows? Maybe Charlie was wounded one time."

"That's a shame."

"Well . . . ducks aren't all that different from people."

"This I have to write down," Bill laughed, taking out his pen and paper. "You, Falcon, can find meaning in just about anything. What a great approach to life! So tell me: How are ducks like people?"

"Well, you've already learned that birds of a feather flock together," Falcon joked. "Let me give you another insight. If they have good experiences, they return to you. If they have bad experiences—like your trip to the French restaurant—they won't be back. One time in which they are not shown empathy is enough to ruin their relationship with people. In ducks, it may be a rock. In humans, it may be a situation where their emotional needs were not recognized. Or worse . . . were ignored."

"I hear you."

"A great German poet and philosopher once wrote that 'Man . . . knows only when he is satisfied and when he suffers, and only his suffering and his satisfactions instruct him concerning himself, teach him what to seek and what to avoid.'"

"Author?"

"Goethe."

"Makes a lot of sense."

"And I'll tell you," Falcon continued, "how we're like monkeys."

"Besides the fact that we're related?"

"Yeah. I mean, how do we learn?"

"Reading? Listening?"

"Doing, Bill. Monkey see, monkey do. We copy, we make mistakes, we learn. Formal teaching may inform and even inspire, but it doesn't show us anything. You learn by being curious, doing, acting. You didn't get good at what you do by sitting in a classroom. The real teacher is life. With small children, they use parents as role models. They model our beliefs, our values, our skills. And as they grow, their environment plays a greater part. Your employees also use you, and each other. *Their* environment."

"But what if we ape someone who's doing it wrong?"

"That's a difficult dilemma. We have to be sensitive to outside signals, and to our intuition—our gut. When you trust yourself, you'll know when the path is taking a detour that's not right for you or your business. Watch small children. They're naturals at reading situations and people."

"Annie seems to have a real ability to charm anyone."

"No . . . I don't mean charm. I mean really reading people. Seeing past the trappings of material success, seeing to the core of people. When my daughter and her husband were going through their divorce, it was very tense, and Annie instinctively knew when to leave the room. Now, some people, my wife for instance, thought this was terrible. And it was sad, but it also showed me how she was honing skills she will use her whole life. She was learning to be aware. The way we made that sadness easier for her was by talking to her, by being open and using good communication skills."

"She seems unscathed."

"Sure. But we all have our private pains. We need to be sensitive to that with adults as well as with children."

"Grandpa! Oh my gosh come here! Come here!!!!" Annie was jumping up and down frantically pointing with excitement at the pond's edge. Falcon and Bill raced to her side.

"You see her? See? There . . . you shoulda seen the . . . there!!!!"

"What honey? Where?"

"There! There!" Annie was pointing so haphazardly that the two men didn't see she was drawing their attention to a small group of baby ducklings hiding in the reeds. Finally, Bill spotted the babies.

"Look, Falcon. There at the water's edge. To the left of that log."

"Shhh!" Falcon urged. The three fell silent and watched as the mother came to tend to her ducklings. After a few moments, Falcon whispered, "Let's give them a little privacy." They moved away and Falcon gave Annie another bag of bread, as he and Bill retreated to their position under the oak tree.

"She was so excited, at first I didn't know what she was pointing at."

"That's my granddaughter. No inhibitions. She's so alive. And you know, when *you* speak to people, you want them to leave with that same kind of enthusiasm. Just energy, pure and simple. People are persuaded by those who show passionate interest."

After Annie had finished with the second bag of bread, she joined the two men. Looking up in their oak tree, she exclaimed, "Grandpa, there's a bluebird up there."

"A blue jay?" Bill asked.

"No. Some other kind of blue bird. I know blue jays. They're mean to the other birds."

Bill and Falcon looked up. Bill squinted, "He's a green bird, Annie. Though I'm not sure what kind of bird either."

"Blue. I can see him perfectly."

Bill insisted, "He's a real deep green. Maybe someone's parakeet got loose."

"Blue." Annie giggled, but she was equally insistent and crossed her arms.

"Green," Bill joked in return.

Falcon said nothing, just walked around the tree several times. Finally, he spoke, "Whoever is *wrong* buys sodas at the snack stand."

"Deal," Annie said confidently.

"Bill, come over here." Bill proceeded over to Falcon, who was now kneeling on the ground. "Lie down right here, where Annie was standing a second ago."

"Lie down? With this suit on?"

"Yup."

Bill felt foolish, but he sat down on the grass and then leaned back to a reclining position. "From this vantage point, the bird *is* blue. I don't believe it."

"Some birds' feathers hit the light different. The sheen changes things. Guess sodas are in order," Falcon laughed heartily as he helped Bill up from the ground.

"Sorry, Annie. I was certain he was green."

Annie took his hand. "That's OK. I knew he was blue all along."

They walked together, Falcon at Bill's side.

"You know what that was called?" Falcon whispered.

"A blue bird?"

"Ethnography."

"Interpret that for me?"

"Walk in another's shoes. In business, you can ask others questions, but you're just going to get an answer from their perspective. What *they* feel at the time. And sometimes they can't even describe it to you. So you have to do what they do. Lie down on the ground and see: *What color is their bird?*"

"I like that. A well-earned soda. Now where to?"

"Sodas. Then the sandbox. You ain't seen nothin' yet."

Bill grinned, Annie's hand tucked in his own. "Falcon, I'm pretty sure you're right!"

BILL'S NOTEPAD

* People respond to smiles. A smile cuts through ego to warmth. Make sure to spread this through the company.

* Children respond when you are genuine and vulnerable to them. So do adults. Let's cut out the pretentious crap and get real in everything we do from advertising, selling . . . to managing, etc.

* Be attentive to our customers' needs. Empathy conveys strength, caring, and composure.

* Everyone must adopt the appropriate caring role when they're with others. This doesn't make that role false. It's simply another side of ourselves.

* People are like ducks. One bad experience can make them back away from us.

* The wisdom of children is in their inability to disguise their feelings. I must be more childlike.

* Heroes are admired because of their strengths—and their weaknesses.

* Excitement is a palpable energy that is contagious. We must always leave our customers with that feeling.

Bill's Notepad

* Monkey see. Monkey do. Our people learn through role models, not through our worn-out rhetoric.

* I must somehow embrace my pain. We learn through suffering.

* I will start trusting my instincts with other people.

* I must get out of my office and actually experience my employees and my customers' perspectives. Always ask myself about others:

* WHAT COLOR IS THEIR BIRD?

Chapter Four

*The heart has its reasons that the mind
cannot comprehend.*

- Plato

✳

At the snack stand, Bill treated Annie to a snow cone, Falcon to a soda, and he got himself a soda and a hot dog smothered in mustard.

"I have to say, this afternoon out of the office has turned out so downright pleasurable I feel guilty," he chuckled half to himself as he savored his junk food. "I never eat hot dogs anymore."

They found a shady picnic table under a tree and watched a nearby boy fly an elaborate trick kite.

"Can I go closer to watch him, Grandpa?"

"Sure Sweetie. Just don't wander off. Stay right there where I can see you."

Annie took her snow cone and approached the boy, who appeared several years older than Annie. He happily showed off for her, making the kite dip and turn.

"You know, Bill," Falcon said, "I've been thinking about our poor duck."

"Yeah . . . me too. Seems such a shame that someone would hurt him."

"Yeah. Trust is a tenuous thing. And you know, I thought of something else about him."

"What's that?"

"Over the winter, we didn't see Charlie. And then this spring, Annie and I have done other things—museum trips, visits to the library—so the duck had no contact with us for a long time. Even if Charlie wasn't abused, he would have been skittish. Ducks need frequency of contact. Just like people."

"You're probably right."

"Think about it. Have you ever had a friend you hadn't seen in a long, long time? Maybe fifteen years. And then you see that your college is having a reunion, or you run into your friend's mother and she urges you to call him. What do you do?"

"Honestly? I'm really uptight. I think 'What if this guy doesn't want to hear from me. We lost touch . . .'"

"Exactly. Me too. And customers are the same. If they don't see us over and over again, they assume the worst. 'I've been forgotten; that company didn't really care about my business; they're just like all the others.' Psychologists say that we have a natural tendency to like that which is familiar to us—that which we deal with over and over and over again. And those things or people we *don't* see . . ."

"I get it. So the lesson is feed the ducks often," Bill joked.

"Something like that. Don't *assume* you are making frequent contact. Guarantee that you are. Let your company be depended on—known for—that kind of connection."

"You know, Falcon, I've been thinking about Annie's blue bird. When I kept trying to insist her bird was a different color, I never succeeded in changing her mind."

"Of course not. It's a waste of time—and in business, a big waste of money—to try to do that with people. We all have too much of ourselves invested in our worldview. Our beliefs, our values, even our prejudices have been established through a lifetime of choices. We can try to be open-minded, but face it, we all make assumptions."

"Like when I assumed my contact would be driving a Porsche, not wearing overalls. What an idiot . . . "

"Not an idiot, just human. We all assume. So the only way we can understand our customers' expectations, anticipate those expectations, make a connection, is by entering into and respecting their way of seeing the world. Children teach us this. That we must acknowledge their feelings—their worldview—before trying to help. Why do we forget and not apply this to adults?"

Falcon was silent for a moment, then continued. "Maybe it's because dealing with people is inherently messy."

"Messy?"

"Sure. In this digital age, marked by e-mail and faxes, it *appears* all neat and tidy. But it's all really a virtual form of communication. Face-to-face communication—real communication— is marked by pacing, attention to body language, voice tone and inflection, more personal contact, more risk—but the rewards are inherently greater. The relationship is—by its very nature—stronger."

Bill finished the last bite of his hot dog and shook his head. "You know, Falcon, I really feel like I've learned a great deal today. I've enjoyed today—enjoyed your granddaughter immensely—but I just think this is all too simple. Anyone can understand this. I need advice that will help me run a hundred-million-dollar corporation . . . that can take me into the future."

Falcon looked disappointed. "So Bill . . . if it's so simple, why isn't everyone doing it? I'll tell you why. Most smart men and women—people like you with your advanced degrees and years of experience—have lost faith in simplicity. You believe that for something to be valuable, it has to be complex. Take how enamored you all are with technology. Now I agree that it can provide you with a competitive advantage . . . but it's temporary. It's simply too easy to copy. You equip all your people with the latest software out in the field. You give them all laptops, cell phones, and palm computers equipped with wireless modems, and make the Internet the corporate savior. But guess what?"

"I know. Tomorrow my number-one competitor is going to give all their people the same state-of-the-art, whizbang sales tools."

"Exactly. But what can't be copied in this technological age is mastering the complex human relationships that remain the bedrock of any business. Empathy and integrity, Bill, cannot be copied."

Annie was by this time holding on to the kite string herself. She was, from their vantage point, having a ball. Soon, however, the wind died and the kite came crashing down. The boy appeared to say something to Annie, and she came running over.

"I don't understand," her lip quivered. "He said he's not going to fly anymore today. The wind went away. But why can't he just run real fast and get the kite up again?"

"Maybe he could, Annie," Bill said, swinging his legs over the seat of the picnic table and squatting next to her. "But then what do you think would happen to the kite when he stopped running?"

"It would fall back down?"

"That's exactly right, Annie! To hold the kite up in the air, the wind has to catch it and float it up there," Bill said gently. "Usually about this time of the day, the wind dies down. The air will be still through nightfall. That's probably it for kite flying today."

Crestfallen, Annie slumped on the picnic bench.

"Weren't we headed for the sandbox anyway?" Bill asked her. "It doesn't matter if the air is still over there."

Annie looked up, a hint of promise in her eyes. "Well? Are we going? Are we?"

The two men smiled and stood.

"To the sandbox!" Bill West joked and raised his arm like a Calvary officer.

"Let's go!" Annie dashed off ahead of them, leading the way.

"Bill . . . I noticed in your kite explanation that you resisted flat out telling Annie the answer. You also didn't try to impress her with how smart you are."

"And your point is?"

"I'm just guessing here, Bill, but I bet sometimes you can't resist letting your customers know that *you're* the expert and that you've figured out the solution to *their* problem. You just have to let them know."

"Well . . ."

"Listen Bill. It's perfectly fine to be wiser than others, if you can. Just make sure you never let them know it. Help them discover the answer on their own, like you did with Annie. Everyone needs to feel smart and empowered. Not just kids."

Bill gazed at the horizon and nodded, as he quietly contemplated his most recent sales presentation.

At the sandbox, Annie approached two children playing with some buckets and shovels, and in no time, the three were playing together happily.

"There's my usual bench," Falcon motioned, and the two men sat down. After a minute or two a tall young woman with blonde hair came over, smiling, to Falcon. She clutched a stack of books in her arms and her backpack looked loaded.

"You don't need to work out, Connie. Just keep lugging those books. Better than weight lifting." Falcon joked.

"You're right, Mr. Falcon. Oh . . . and I checked out that book by Voltaire. Thanks. It was just what I needed for my report."

"Connie, this is Bill West, a friend of mine."

"I'd shake your hand, Mr. West, but I'm a little loaded down," Connie had an easy smile. "If you're all set here, Mr. Falcon, I'm going to go. I need to hit the library."

"Not enough books?"

"Very funny," she grinned and turned and headed toward the parking lot.

"She's the babysitter for those two children. They're on Annie's soccer team, and I watch them on Thursdays for an hour or so when their sitter's schedule doesn't perfectly overlap with their parents' work schedules."

"Annie plays soccer? Great sport."

"Yeah. And she's pretty good too. Then again she has a great coach."

"Don't tell me . . ."

Falcon laughed out loud. "You're lookin' at him!"

The two men sat watching the children. Bill took out his pen and notebook, "Let me take a few minutes to scribble a note or two. I'm telling you, I haven't felt this energized in a while."

Falcon smiled. "Good. Me? I'm going to watch these kids at play. Look at Annie. She hasn't looked over at us once," Falcon spoke quietly. "Look at how they're all getting along. Me? I'm out of sight, out of mind."

"Does that hurt your feelings a little?"

"No. It's as it should be. And you know, our customers do that, too. We humans are a pretty predictable bunch."

"What are they doing now?"

The other little girl and boy and Annie were lying down in the sand and moving their arms and legs. Then the three of them stood up.

"Sand angels!" They screamed in unison.

Bill and Falcon shared a hearty laugh.

"Now I've seen everything," Bill chuckled.

"Well, they certainly are creative. Then again, they don't have the same inhibitions as we do. They're not afraid of getting dirty or looking a little foolish."

"They're covered in sand! Look at Annie's hair!"

"Cute, huh? My car is going to be full of sand tonight. But, I recall a great thinker who once said, 'Genius is childhood recaptured at will.'

"Well, they are little geniuses. Making 'snow' angels in the sand."

"We think that kind of creativity and imagination is great when you're seven. But when you get into corporate culture, everyone's afraid to play. Afraid to look foolish or make a mistake. We have a tendency to be so serious. We look down on spontaneity and child-like ingenuity."

"I guess that goes along with what you were saying about people at the top, thinking solutions can't be simple."

"Precisely."

The two men sat in silence, watching the three children playing. Suddenly, an argument appeared to break out over one of the sand tools they were using to construct an elaborate castle.

"Should we go help them sort it out?" Bill asked.

"No. I try to let Annie learn how to manage her own feelings."

Annie abruptly stood up, folded her arms across her chest and stomped her way over to Falcon. She was angry, but both Falcon and Bill could hear the frustration in her voice.

"I had it first and Mike said I could use it, and then Jessica took it away from me and it's not even hers!"

Falcon soothed his granddaughter with gentle words about the difficulties of sharing and the importance of compromise.

"Couldn't you offer to let Jessica use it for five minutes and then you could use it?" Bill asked. "I could let you know when five minutes is up. I could set my watch alarm."

"I guess I could," Annie shrugged. She wiped her face with the back of her hand and went back over to her playmates. Soon, peace seemed to reign in the sandbox again.

"See how you didn't vilify the other children, Bill?"

"Hmm?" Bill was setting his watch alarm.

"You didn't tell Annie, 'Gosh, that other little girl is so mean or selfish.'"

"Well, no, it's just kid stuff."

"Kid stuff, huh? Unique to kids, right?

"Exactly."

"So, with children, we should hear anger as pain or as frustration. We shouldn't hear it as anger. We also shouldn't let it draw us in. But with adults, it's different?"

"I never really thought about it that way."

"Bill. How often do you do that in business? Get drawn into the middle of something that really is best resolved with a healthy dose of empathy?"

"I have a tendency to get in the cross fire between my people. And you're right. I hear how angry they are. I hear rage sometimes—desk-pounding screaming fits. But what I don't hear are those sandbox clues."

"Sandbox clues," Falcon grinned. "Now you're the one coming up with this stuff. What are sandbox clues?"

"Well, in some ways, my people are acting like kids in a sandbox. At times, they have a desperate need to be heard or understood, just like Annie did. But I don't hear that. I hear it as a full-scale war, and I have to get involved. You know Falcon, I suppose the same thing can happen with angry customers or suppliers."

"And?"

"And . . . I have to make sure that my people slow down. Tune the world out—including their own emotional reactions—and tune our customers in. We must genuinely care about the pain or fear or whatever emotion is behind that anger. Again, those sandbox clues."

"I like that insight Bill."

Bill's alarm went off and he shouted over to the sandbox. "Time to switch."

Peace continued in the sandbox.

"I wish all my people's conflicts were so simple to resolve."

"They can be. If we contain it in the sandbox and don't let it spill over."

"I hear you."

The two men continued watching the children, but Bill West's mind was churning in circles. Could it all be this simple? Had he simply forgotten those qualities of genuineness, empathy, vulnerability, and creativity? Could he do as Falcon urged? Could he recapture his childhood at will?

BILL'S NOTEPAD

* Frequency ensures comfort. Make sure our people are maintaining contact with our customers. Feed the ducks often—our new mantra.

* Be wiser than our customers—but help them arrive at solutions. Don't try to point out just how wise we are.

* Empathy and integrity can't be copied. That has to be our competitive edge.

* Out of sight, out of mind. Remain in sight of our customers.

* Encourage child-like ingenuity and creativity in the workplace.

* It's easier to empathize with children, but we must make our empathy with adults run just as deeply and sincerely. It's more important to be kind, than it is to be right!

* Watch for sandbox clues during all communications, especially conflicts.

CHAPTER FIVE

*The truth is more important
than the facts.*

- Frank Lloyd Wright

✳

*B*ill West found himself staring at the clouds floating above the playground. He knew, on any other day, despite his corner office with its magnificent view of the city, he wouldn't have noticed the skyline, let alone the sky. He would have been concentrating on his spreadsheets; answering phone calls in rapid-fire succession. He would never have seen the perfect white clouds overhead.

The sky, he decided, looked surreal; dreamlike. The blue was too clear, too crisp, too perfectly . . . blue. Not even a master like Michelangelo, not even the Sistine Chapel he had marveled at two years ago on a trip to Italy, could duplicate the perfection of nature's masterpiece. Each cloud was so fluffy it looked as if it was made of the softest spun cotton. The air was so clean and crisp, and there were no sounds of phone lines jangling, people talking, footsteps pounding across office floors as employees raced to and fro. No, the sounds were of children laughing and the wind rustling leaves.

He shut his eyes for a moment and was transported back to his own childhood. He recalled one day lying out on the grass in the shadow of his grandfather's big oak tree. Golden sunlight darting through green leaves. His cousin Lily and he were flat on their backs staring up at the sky. Hours passed with no more than a few words between them. Their conversation was as simple as "Don't you think that cloud looks like a bear?" "Yup." "Can you see that robin's nest?" "I wonder how many eggs she's laid." Childhood . . . time had a way of slipping past him, a way of escaping from his grasp. He forgot about robin's nests and picture-perfect days you swear you'd never forget. Skies so blue you were sure you'd stared at them so long that they were ingrained in your brain forever. Perhaps they were, Bill mused, but then the world got in the way and you had a tendency to forget them. He certainly had. Suddenly, he felt profoundly reminiscent. Falcon jolted him from his mood, but it was as if he was reading Bill's mind.

"What would you have been if you hadn't gone into business?" Falcon directed his question to Bill as both their gazes ventured to the children playing in the sandbox.

Bill took a moment to collect his thoughts. "Honestly?" he said, recalling talks he and Lily had shared about what they would each become when they grew up. "If I wasn't so driven, I probably would have done something to help animals. My wife and I have been to Africa three times, and ever since I was a kid, I've loved animals. Would have been a vet, but I was lousy in biology."

"You have any pets?"

"A few. We've got two dogs—an Akita, and a loveable mutt who wandered into our lives six years ago and never left. My wife has had her cat for fourteen years—an old, fat tabby named Mac. And we have a couple of canaries."

"A regular menagerie."

"Yeah. You could say that. It's a side of me people don't ordinarily see. But with what you've said about making yourself vulnerable . . . perhaps it's a side people *should* see."

"I think so. It's like Annie here. Even before I sold the company, when she was just a baby, I used to bring her into the office from time to time, show her off. Can you tell I'm the proudest grandfather on the planet? The days she came in reminded all of us in the company that we're human. Even the CEO gets down on his hands and knees and crawls around with the baby—and there's nothing wrong with that. We should be vulnerable. We don't have to be gods to our employees."

"Like the Greek heroes you referred to earlier."

"Exactly."

"What about you, Falcon? What would you have done if you hadn't been a captain of industry?"

"Me? I would have been a magician."

"A magician?"

"Yup. Then I could've spent all of my time playing with children—small ones like Annie there, and big kids, like me!"

With that, Falcon bounded off the bench and sprang onto his hands. "Ha!" he shouted, "I can still do a handstand!" He held his pose for another moment before righting himself again.

"You know any magic tricks?"

"Do I know any magic tricks? Watch, my friend. And remember two words: truth and fact."

"Truth and fact? They're the same thing, aren't they?"

"Far from it, Bill. Far from it."

With that, Falcon strode over to the children. He sat on the wooden edge of the sandbox, with his feet in the sand and gathered Mike, Jessica, and Annie around his knees.

His first trick was every grandfather's favorite. He pulled a silver dollar from his pocket and made it disappear. Then he pulled it out of Mike's ear, much to the children's delight.

"Do it again! Do it again!" They screamed in unison.

Falcon happily obliged, pulling a silver dollar out of Jessica's ear, then Annie's. The children poked and probed in both ears, as if more coins were hidden there.

"You know," Falcon said, "I suppose you each need a silver dollar." With that he took a white handkerchief out of his other pocket. Then he squeezed and tugged at his nose with elaborate and loud sound effects that drove the children into fits of laughter. Suddenly, with a shocked expression on his face, three coins appeared in his handkerchief. "These must belong to each of you," he said as he handed the large, shiny coins to his audience.

"OK kids, now for this trick I need an assistant. Or maybe three assistants." He picked up a handful of sand and slowly poured it into his clenched fist. He held his fist out in front of each of the children and one by one he had them blow on his hand.

"Now for the magic words: SwamiWamiYooHoo."

Jessica shrieked with laughter. "What? What kind of magic words are those?"

"They're special magic words."

"You're supposed to say Abracadabra," Mike chimed in.

50

"Not this magician. Now all together: SwamiWamiYoo HOO!!!!!"

The children shouted out the magic words, and with a flourish, Falcon opened his hand.

"The sand disappeared!" Mike grabbed Falcon's hand and stared at it. "How'd you do that?"

"A good magician never reveals his secrets." Falcon stood and bowed to his audience. Annie and her friends cheered loudly.

When Falcon rejoined Bill on the bench, Bill clapped. "Bravo! Not bad for an amateur magician, there, Falcon. I know the old coin-in-the-ear trick, but I have to admit I'm not sure how you did the sand trick."

"It's all about perception."

"I sense I'm about to learn something profound here," Bill ribbed his new friend.

"Actually Bill, it's not deep at all. I simply want to remind you that there is often a big difference between the facts—what you believe or know about your company or products—and your audience's truth, or their perception."

"Like your magic trick."

"Precisely. You see, the truth is that the kids all saw the sand go into my fist. The truth is what's believed. The *fact* was that the sand never really did go into my hand. But what those kids believe—their truth—is far more important than facts. Their perception is that I can make sand disappear. They believe it. That makes it so."

"Heck, I believed it." Bill smiled.

"Do you like magic?"

"Yeah. I actually do."

"Hold out your hand."

Falcon grabbed Bill's wrist, turned his palm face up and poured sand from his seemingly empty fist onto Bill's hand.

"OK, now I am thoroughly in awe. This sand seems awfully real to me."

"Listen, Bill. You and I both know magic always boils down to some kind of trick. And while we might have fun trying to figure out how the magician made the elephant disappear—or made the sand appear out of thin air—we *love* it when we can't figure it out. When we can believe in the magic and be transported for a few minutes or an hour or whatever. And I liken magic to marketing."

"Smoke and mirrors?"

"Not smoke and mirrors. You're not trying to *fool* anyone. I mean emotionally involving your customers. Getting them so involved in your message that they forget that they are being marketed to. Face it. People know you're trying to sell something to them, just as the magician's audience knows they are about to watch a trick. But people want to get lost in the marketing. They want it to be invisible. They want to get lost in your marketing, just like the audience wants to get lost in the performance. So, the best marketing or sales is like the best performance. Your audience feels the benefit, rather than it being overt or obvious."

"Sure. You don't want your marketing to be dull."

"But it's more than that, Bill. I have an example of classic customer perception at work. Their truth is their subjective reality. An airline executive once noted that passengers assumed that if their seat pockets or tray tables were dirty, perhaps the airline also did a poor job of servicing their engines."

"Not a very logical inference."

"Logic has nothing to do with it. That's why you have slogans like 'Fly the Friendly Skies', not 'We Fly Safe Planes.' It's about subtlety. Entering the psyche through the subconscious mind. Discovering and making mental connections."

"Subjective reality."

"That's the *only* reality, Bill. How about the story of the two competing neighborhood candy stores. Everything was pretty much the same at both establishments—same selection, same prices, same quality—but the neighborhood kids preferred one store over the other."

"The difference was the service, huh?" Bill interjected.

Falcon smiled. "Well . . . to an extent. But not the way you're probably thinking. Both owners were extremely friendly, and responsive. The problem was one of *truth* versus *fact*. You see, when the kids were asked why they preferred one store over the other they replied, 'Because the lady in the 'good' store always gives us extra candy. The lady in the 'bad' store always takes candy away.'"

Bill looked at Falcon with a puzzled expression. "Wait a minute, Falcon. I thought you said everything was the same at both stores. You didn't say that one store gave out extra candy with each order."

Falcon laughed. "The *fact*, Bill, is that the lady in the 'good' store *didn't* give extra candy. She simply put a small amount of candy on the scale and slowly kept adding to it. On the other hand, the lady in the 'bad' store would pile a heaping load of candy on the scale and then take candy away until she reached the correct weight. The facts—same amount of candy—didn't matter to the kids. Only their *truth* mattered. So, Bill, the lesson is . . . "

"I must make sure to always *add* to my customers' experience?"

Falcon smiled. "That too. But this particular lesson is that the key to successful marketing is to discover your customers' *truths*. What they feel is true. If you discover, uncover, and satisfy their unique emotional needs, you will, in their subjective reality, be the company, the salesperson, the supplier they want to do business with."

"This I'm jotting down," Bill said, pulling out his trusty pen.

Falcon paused. "You ready for a little shocker?"

"Sure," Bill said, pen poised.

"You know the golden rule? Do unto others . . . "

" . . . as you would have them do unto you. Absolutely. Who could forget it?"

"I want *you* to, Bill. I want you to never, *ever* follow the golden rule in a business setting with your customers."

"What?!"

"I'm serious. What makes you think that what *you* want or how *you* want to be treated is the same for them? Instead, you must do unto your customers as they *uniquely* want done unto them. Give them exactly what they want, any way they want it. Serve them the way *they* want to be served. The intangible benefits of emotions and feelings will be realized."

"I got you."

"And when we talked about making all communication count, that holds true here. Whatever the source of contact— face-to-face, telephone, electronic, written word—creating positive feelings is your job. It's the essence of the relationship."

"It's not simply about all the market analysis I've paid for. It's deeper than that."

"Absolutely, Bill. We're more than statistics and analysis. We're hearts as much as heads. Actually, we're hearts first, and then heads. People make decisions emotionally—Is it relevant? Is it me? Do I trust them?—and then, and only then, do they deal with the rational—features, attributes, pricing."

"I hear you. It's like buying a car. First you decide what kind of car you want—the snazzy red sports car, the sedan, the van. The decision is as much emotional as it is rational."

"It's virtually *all* emotion, Bill. Like you baby boomers. You all own those 4-wheel drive, sport utility vehicles, but no one ever drives the darn things off road."

"Hmm."

"Or the semi-retired millionaire indulging his passion for classic cars. When I buy a car, it's more about the memories or the evocative nature of what that car meant to me as a young boy than it is about what kind of 'deal' I'm getting. It's the emotions sparked by the vehicle."

Bill nodded, "Sure. So once we decide with our heart what we want and—especially relevant to our conversation—where we want to buy and who we want to buy from, then we use our head to punch the numbers. Do I want four cylinders or six? Do I want to lease or own? Do I want the extended warrantee? Am I getting a good deal?"

"And when heart and head meet, at that juncture the purchase is made."

The two men pondered their conversation as Annie slowly walked towards Falcon with Mike and Jessica following right on her heels. All three children had devious grins on their little faces.

"Love you!" She kissed him on the cheek.

"Love you too, Sweet Pea."

"Tag," she tapped his arm. "You're it!"

Laughing, all three children dashed off in different directions, kicking up a cloud of dust behind them. Falcon stood and started jogging after Annie.

"Come on, Bill, help me."

Bill smiled and looked down at his serious wing-tip shoes.

"Oh boy," he said, "another adventure." And with that he ran after Falcon and Annie, her long black hair streaming in back of her, and squeals and shrieks of laughter echoing through the park.

Bill's Notepad

* Perception is truth.

* Our marketing and selling shouldn't be overt. Let our customers get lost in our own brand of magic.

* Subjective reality has its own set of rules. Customers' reality—their truth—is what's important. We can't forget that.

* Make sure to always add to our customers' experience with us.

* Do not follow the Golden Rule. Instead, seek understanding and then give customers what they want. What they uniquely want!

CHAPTER SIX

From error to error,
one discovers the truth.

- Sigmund Freud

✱

*B*ill was undermined, he decided, by his wing-tip shoes. The three children darted behind trees and crawled on their bellies beneath bushes. Falcon wasn't afraid to join them, either. The knees of his overalls were covered in grass stains.

Not in this suit, Bill mused, as he tried to avoid young Jessica's grasp. But, try as he might, and despite the fact that he was once a pretty fair long-distance runner in college, Bill found himself the dreaded "It" for most of the game of tag.

Bill huddled over, trying to catch his breath. Falcon came within three feet of him, as the children fanned out and scattered.

"Now Bill, I realize we've covered a lot of ground today—no pun intended—but I'm only going to stand this close to you. And I'm not going to let you catch me," Falcon smirked playfully.

Bill inhaled deeply, "I don't get it. . . . I used to be able to run circles around anybody."

"Circles Bill, or straight ahead? See, this game is a lot like the marketplace today."

"Don't tell me you've found a way to make tag a lesson, Falcon."

"The biggest. Competition is global—no boundaries—and lightening fast. Technology changes at the speed of light. Knowledge is growing exponentially. We suddenly have *too* much information. So what does all that tell you?"

"Not to play tag in serious shoes," Bill joked, looking down at his now-muddied dress shoes.

"True. Dress shoes . . . heck, they're a metaphor for serious business. But now the corporate culture requires quick reflexes. Athletic shoes, if you will. Look at me," with that, Falcon lifted his foot up. "I got me some 'serious sneakers.' All the better to make me agile, flexible, quick on my feet. And Bill?"

"Yeah?"

"You're still it!" Falcon laughed as he took off across the field with the children.

Bill stopped for a moment. *All this requires is some thought*, he mused. *Who's the weakest runner?* He watched as the children dashed back and forth. He decided that both girls were light on their feet, but Mike was a little slower, and he seemed to get winded more easily. Bill ran off toward Mike.

"Okay, there Buddy, I'm going to catch you," Bill laughed as he drew closer to Mike, who was now laughing and screaming at the same time.

"No way! No way!" Mike shouted over his shoulder. Just as Bill was within inches of him, Mike cut sharply to his right and hopped over a puddle, escaping and catching up to Annie.

"HA! I got away!" Mike yelled out.

Falcon again came within a few feet of Bill.

"Remember the path to success, Bill? That stuff about the customer's truth?"

"Yeah," Bill hunched over, again catching his breath and feeling a twinge in his right knee.

"Well, it changes just like Mike. In an instant and without warning, the customer can be demanding something else entirely—can head off in another direction. And all we can do is try to anticipate and if we don't anticipate the change ahead of time, then we better react. Instantly. Or we'll be in a mud puddle while our competition catches them. And then our *competition* will have our customer's loyalty, and we'll just be another runner in the pack."

Bill remained hunched over, hands on his knees. "Maybe there's a lesson here. Or maybe I'm just too old for tag."

"Nonsense. You're just thinking too much. Why'd you choose Mike?"

"He stops more often than the girls to catch his breath."

"Nice try. But remember there's a danger in choosing a single direction. Maybe you assumed something that wasn't true. Maybe it was the wrong plan."

"Obviously. I'm over here, and he's way over there. That's *my* truth."

"Well, as Winston Churchill said, 'Man will occasionally stumble over the truth, but usually manages to pick himself up, walk around it, and carry on.' There's truth here on the field, Bill. You're just ignoring it. In tag, as in business, you have to be willing to get messy."

"Messy?"

"To look for shortcuts. To take chances. Take risks, Bill. Get a few grass stains on the knees. It's just a truth you don't like because of your suit and sensible shoes. The truth is you have to take risks. Listen . . . you have a lot of finger-pointing in your company?"

"Doesn't every company? It's not marketing's fault, it's manufacturing's. It's the manager of the sales division. It's the consultant. It's the guy who sells bagels in the morning. It's everyone else's fault."

"But that's not true of *every* company, is it, Bill?"

"No. Not in companies that are hitting all their numbers."

"That's not true. They still finger-point. And if they don't finger-point, they slap themselves on the back and say 'Me! Me! I did it single-handedly.'"

"Human nature."

"No. I refuse to believe that. I call it a Disease of Inertia."

"Hmm?" Bill stood up and wiped his brow.

"You don't typically see those problems in an entrepreneurial company. Why not?"

"Too busy trying to get started."

"That's just a tiny part of it. No . . . entrepreneurial companies thrive on innovation; on change. The leader is totally market driven. He or she doesn't give a damn about seniority, operational status quo, looking foolish . . . the leader focuses solely on the customer and doing whatever it takes to woo, win, and keep that customer, regardless of whose toes are stepped on or the discomfort it creates."

"Great. But we're not a startup anymore. We've got hundreds of employees and a pretty complex business on our hands."

"I didn't say 'startup'. I said 'entrepreneurial'. Hell, even the best big and complex companies are still entrepreneurial. They all have *very* detailed plans yet are still flexible. They're continually introducing new products or trying various distribution channels, searching for the right direction. Changing, testing. Testing, measuring. The key is for the leader—you, Bill—to create an environment that rewards innovation. One that *embraces* failure, instead of simply tolerating it. Let your people see *you* make mistakes. Make it safe for them to do the same."

"That makes a lot of sense, Falcon. As long as they don't make the same mistake twice. Right?"

"Wrong Bill. We're talking about a very complex, rapidly changing environment. People are going to make the same mistakes over and over until they become proficient at—and especially comfortable with—the *new* ways of doing business. If you discourage or punish mistakes, you'll be discouraging experimentation, learning and change. The very disciplines that will keep you in business."

"Hey, you two!" Annie shouted across the field, "Stop talking and start running!"

"Remember, Bill, take risks," Falcon smiled and darted off.

Bill took off after the three kids and Falcon. His feet hurt and his old football knee was reminding him of the time he was tackled while trying to score on a naked bootleg.

"Hey kids! Why don't we play Red Rover? Aren't you tired of tag?"

"No! No!" The three kids shouted back.

"Hey Bill!" Falcon cupped his hands, "Customer innovation demands zigs and zags like tag. You have to make things happen, rather than wait for them to happen. Constantly improve, evolve, grow. Forget about the old 'barriers to entry' game. No one's standing still for Red Rover anymore. Exhausting?"

"Yes!" Bill shouted back.

"If you're going to innovate to achieve customer loyalty, you have to be clever . . . and quicker."

Bill saw Jessica inching her way toward him as if to tease him a bit. He pretended not to notice her, and then he feigned left, then right, then left again and tried to catch her. Unfortunately, his knee didn't cooperate and he crashed to the ground.

"Bill? You OK?" Falcon trotted over.

"You OK, Mr. West?" Annie asked as the three kids approached the fallen businessman.

"Just a bruised ego."

"Maybe we should stop, kids," Falcon offered.

"Sure, sure, Mr. West. We can stop."

Bill looked up at the four faces now surrounding him. He turned deadly serious and growled, "Not on your life!!" Suddenly he popped up and winked. "No mercy now," he grinned broadly.

The children ran off, but Falcon remained. "You sure you're OK?"

"It dawned on me as I brushed *mud* off my face, Falcon, I need to play to win. I can't worry about this suit or my damn serious shoes. Just like if I'm going to turn the company around, I can't worry about playing a flawless game. Instead, I have to assess constantly. Change rapidly. Make mistakes and move on. Just move, period!"

"George Wald once said, 'We are the products of editing, rather than of authorship.'"

"Well, watch out. Bill West is back in the game!"

Falcon took off downfield, and Bill surveyed the landscape. A large clump of oleander bushes blocked Jessica and Annie from his view. He jogged toward the bushes. The girls were giggling behind them. *They think I'm going to go around*, Bill thought to himself. In a single, perfectly executed movement, he dove beneath the bushes. Branches scratched at him, and he felt mud seeping through the knees of his suit. But he found his target. His left hand grabbed Annie's right sneaker.

"You're 'It,'" he shouted as his head peeked through the branches.

"Yikes!" she squealed and took off after Jessica.

The game progressed for nearly a half-hour as they all ran around the field. Bill could not remember the last time he had sweat or laughed so much.

"Hey kids," Falcon called out, "How about giving a couple of old men a rest? Let's meet at the big oak tree for some story telling."

"YAY!" The kids shouted.

Bill leaned over, sweat dripping from his forehead, breath heaving. "'Play to win,' Falcon says. 'Don't be afraid of getting messy.' My drycleaner is going to make a killing on my next order," he looked down at his suit.

"OK, so maybe we took the lesson a bit too literally," Falcon smiled, "but business is about trusting your gut. Rules. I love 'em and I hate 'em. I'm not sure there's a rule about not diving under bushes to catch your opponent, but if there is, it was meant to be broken. Beautiful play, by the way."

"Thank you, Coach." Bill ran his hands through his sopping wet hair.

"If you identify your vision in business, Bill, you'll know when to break the rules. You'll say the heck with the status quo, we're moving forward. Trust your guts, trust your instincts. There's a big difference between following rules and being mindful of principles. So go ahead. Create and adapt. Textbooks can inform you, but they can't teach you this stuff. Remember what I said when we first met today? It's all about your experience. Not what I *tell* you, but what you *feel*."

"I *feel* wiped out."

"But there's no complacency in tag. You can't flounder mid-field hoping one of the kids will dart by so you can catch 'em."

"That's for sure. Hope had nothing to do with it. This was about surviving."

"Being nimble on your feet."

"Forgetting serious shoes."

"Donning cross-trainers."

"I must have looked like an idiot out there."

"We don't grow by having the answers, Bill. We grow by living the questions. You must be forever searching. And being in sync with our customers—following their lead like following those kids over there—means the occasional mud bath."

Bill suddenly roared with laughter. "Will you look at this shirt? It was white when I left the house this morning."

"You've changed today, Bill."

"I feel that old passion again, Falcon. I sure am changing."

"Change is the key, Bill. Follow the words of Mahatma Gandhi and 'Become the change you want to see in others.'"

The two men arrived at the oak tree where all three kids were lying on their backs, cheeks still flush from the game of tag.

"Story time, kids," Falcon said and got down on the ground with them.

Bill shrugged. "Suit's already ruined," Bill said and settled down on the dirt right next to them.

BILL'S NOTEPAD

* Business is messy and always a little out of control.

* Fail. Fail often. But we should fail our way into the future, learning as we go.

* I must embrace failure, not simply tolerate it.

* Play to win!

* Be willing to change directions, to zig and zag as our customers need us to.

* Effective leaders don't worry about the status quo.

* Discovering the truth is an unending journey.

CHAPTER SEVEN

It turns out human beings reason by
means of stories, not by mounds of data.

- Tom Peters

✳

*M*ike, Jessica, and Annie, rosy-cheeked and slightly out of breath gathered in a semi-circle around Falcon and Bill. They were in the shade of a massive oak tree and Annie was gathering acorns in her vicinity and lining them up in front of her.

"You ready kids?" Falcon asked, sitting cross-legged, hands on his knees.

The three children yelled gleefully, "Story time! Story time!"

"OK," Falcon winked at Bill.

Bill smiled, "Finally, a rest from all the lessons."

"What do you mean 'a rest'?" Falcon asked.

"What do you mean, what do I mean? What does telling stories have to do with corporate America? With my slumping sales figures?"

"Bill," Falcon chided, "all this sweating and grass stains, ice cream, and birds, and you haven't picked up on it yet? Lao-Tse wrote it years ago . . . wise men hear and see as little children do. There's value for you in *every* experience, if you're aware. But you need to understand that, Bill. When you leave me today, I won't be there to push your thinking into different dimensions. It will be up to you to make connections in your mind where none existed before."

"I understand," said Bill, as Annie and her friends continued stockpiling acorns.

"Do you, Bill? This isn't some kind of pop management theory. It's a way of being. The knowledge you need to succeed will come only from the different perspectives you gain. The perspectives you gain *outside* your company. *Outside* your comfort zone."

"Okay. I hear you. I understood about Annie's bird. About the zigging and zagging in tag. But storytelling?"

Falcon turned his attention towards the children and assured them that he'd only be a minute or two more. "Bill, let me ask you a few quick questions. First, do you want your company to compete in the marketplace by having the lowest prices?"

"Of course not. That's not a profitable long-term strategy. What good would lowballing do?"

"OK. Here's the next one. Are you finding it more and more difficult to find the right people when hiring?"

"Come on, Falcon. You know these are rhetorical questions. Your point?"

"My point, Bill, is that to compete for customers or the best employees, you need to differentiate yourself. You must offer them a value that they'll pay a premium for or go out of their way for. Make sense?"

"Sure. That's why people pay $4.00 for a cup of gourmet coffee now—when they used to get a bottomless cup for less than a buck. About the same cost, for the beans and all . . ."

"Right, but now they'll even drive out of their way for that *differentiated* cup."

"I'm with you."

"Good. And Bill, would you also agree that this is especially important in today's marketplace which is supersaturated with choice and inundated with information?"

"Sure. I'd go for that, too."

"OK. So you need to be *known* for something. Or to use business jargon—you need a strong *brand*. A strong product brand. A strong company brand. It's a necessity. Any guess as to what makes a *great* brand, Bill?" Falcon raised his eyebrows.

"Alright, Falcon. I'm starting to see these from a mile off. Storytelling?" Bill replied, flashing a broad smile at Falcon.

"Good deduction. See Bill, the great brand *is* a story. It's not about rattling off features and benefits. It's about meaning and feelings—"

"Because we're all in the feelings business!" Bill chuckled.

"Bill, you are a quick study. Yes . . . the feelings business. And how do we connect to our customers' and employees' feelings? Through stories. Stories that move them. Stories that connect with their hearts, with their aspirations. Like I said during tag, the pace of change and sweeping technological advances have all but eliminated traditional strategic advantages. You know . . . those barriers of entry that you learned about in business school, like economies of scale and control of distribution. Red Rover is over, Bill. A great brand and its growing relationship with customers and employees are really your only remaining strategic advantages. Get it?"

"Got it!"

"Good. Now let's tell these kids some stories before they steal every squirrel's acorn under this tree!"

Falcon turned to the three children who now settled down from their acorn hoarding and were wide-eyed with anticipation. "So who has a story to share with me and Bill today?"

Mike started waving his hand wildly in the air. Falcon playfully pretended he didn't see Mike's excitement.

"What? No one has a story today? I can't believe it! You kids *always* have stories. But I guess this is going to be one of those days—"

Mike could stand it no longer, "I do! I do, Mr. Falcon!"

"Oh. Mike? Mike has a story. I didn't even see his hand up there."

The children all giggled. "Story please," Annie said, as this was clearly a ritual the children enjoyed.

"Well . . . today I was wicked nervous when I left for school. Today . . . was . . ." Mike whispered, " . . . report card day."

"And?" said Bill.

"And last night I dreamed three monsters came to get me. Not just any monsters. Huge scary looking monsters with big fangs and lots of hair. And green teeth. And big glow-in-the-dark red eyes. And this morning, I peeked under my bed for those monsters, but they weren't there. So I knew they were waiting for me at school. I thought I saw them behind every tree. And in the principal's office. I was sure I saw one hiding in the cafeteria. The monsters were everywhere until I got my report card. And then . . . when I opened my report card—"

"Yes?" said Jessica expectantly.

"They disappeared. Poof." Mike gazed skyward and made a flourish with his hands. "Because . . . I got three A's and two B's."

Falcon slapped his knee. "That's the best news, Mike. The best! You should be very proud of yourself. That's quite a leap from last year."

Mike nodded, grinning broadly. "I've got brains in every corner of my head."

"You sure do, Mike. Congratulations." Bill said, as the two little girls each gave Mike a high-five.

When everyone had settled down, Falcon spoke. "So tell me, Mike, what do you think made the difference this year?"

"You know how you're always telling us to believe in ourselves, Mr. Falcon?"

Falcon nodded.

"Well, this year it's a lot easier to do that. I like myself a lot better with my new teacher."

"Your new teacher?" asked Bill.

Falcon interjected, "Sure. A teacher is the CEO of the classroom. He or she has the power to make the children believe they can do it. Believe it's right there—within their grasp. The magic monster potion."

"I could use some of that monster potion myself."

"That magic monster potion is yours to have Bill. Simply combine mutual respect with a lot of open communication, and a healthy dose of supportive leadership. I call it spirit enhancement. Don't squash a child's spirit—or a child-like spirit—nurture it."

"Isn't this getting a little touchy-feely?"

"Not at all. We're in the—"

Bill laughed in spite of himself, "The feelings business. OK. I think I got that one."

"Do you Bill? Feelings . . . what's another word we can use? We keep coming back to this point. Maybe feelings make us—in the business world—a little uncomfortable. How about passion? You see Bill, only the passions—and the passionate—have the ability to inspire, to persuade. And when you're passionate, how do you communicate with others? You tell a story. A personal anecdote. You wave your arms about like Mike there. Memos, e-mail, PowerPoint? Those aren't going to inspire or convince anyone of anything. Would William Wallace of Elerslie—"

"Braveheart, right?"

Falcon nodded, "Would he have defeated Longshank's armies by sitting his men down on a hill and giving them some long-winded, albeit beautifully polished, presentation? With all the practiced pauses that so many professional speakers have down just so? No. He spoke from the heart. He expressed his views in a passionate way; in a storytelling way. And they became engaged. And Wallace developed an intimate relationship with them. And they believed . . . and they defied the odds and conquered evil."

"From the heart."

"Always from the heart. You try. Tell the kids a story."

"I'm not very good at this sort of thing."

"Sure you are. It's a lot easier than you think."

"PLEEEEASE!!!!!!" A chorus of voices urged him on.

Bill sighed. *First tag, now fairy tales. I'm not sure about this. I can't even entertain my nephew for ten minutes.* "OK. Here goes." He looked at the upturned faces, then down at the ground. And suddenly, a story from his childhood flew into his mind.

"Hand me that acorn, Annie." She complied and handed him the smallest acorn on her pile.

"See this acorn?"

The children nodded.

"This acorn's name is Arnie. And Arnie is the smallest acorn in the park. In fact, he is so small that he might be the smallest acorn on record anywhere. We're talking Guinness Book of World Records small. But Arnie's parents always told him, 'Arnie, have no fear because deep within you is the potential to be the biggest oak in the forest. A giant among trees.'"

"Of course, Arnie heard this, but he didn't really believe it because a lot of the other acorns made fun of him. They told him he was too scrawny to ever amount to anything. But Arnie's father, the mightiest oak in the park, told him not to worry. And after a while, Arnie stopped listening to the other acorns. Instead, he listened to the still, small acorn voice inside of himself that told him 'You can become a giant oak, Arnie, if only you believe.'"

Bill found himself drawn into his own story. He was changing his voice to the character of Arnie.

"And so, one spring, after a long, cold, snowy winter, Arnie set down his roots. He told himself, 'Believe, Arnie. Believe.' By now, the other acorn voices were a distant echo. And sure enough, he felt himself growing tall." Bill stood and stretched his hands towards the clouds.

"With each passing year, his roots grew deeper into the earth, and he felt connected to every living thing. Soon, he was nudging above all the other trees until finally . . . finally . . . he was the tallest in the park. By then, he was very wise, and often little acorns came to him for advice and wisdom. And always, always, Arnie took the time to tell them his own life story. 'You can be mighty,' he told them. 'You can become a giant, if only you believe.' And Arnie lived happily ever after."

The children clapped and cheered their approval.

"That was the *best* story," said Jessica, as Annie and Mike nodded their approval.

Bill glanced at Falcon, suddenly self-conscious. He shrugged, "It was the best I could do on short notice."

"That was great! You see Bill, the best stories aren't necessarily long-winded or once-upon-a-time tales. And they don't have to be humorous with some big punch line. Story-telling is really just a way to express your message so that it comes alive. Sometimes a story is just a memorable one-liner with the power to remain in your client's mind long after you've gone on to your next client. Sometimes it's a powerful image, like the best advertising. But the greatest stories, Bill, are those that excite the imagination and engage the listener. And I think you did that very well. Our friends here were plenty engaged. They'll never forget little Arnie . . . or you, Bill."

"Thanks, Falcon."

"And Bill?"

"Ya, Falcon."

Falcon reached over and grabbed him tightly around the shoulder. "Don't forget," he added, grinning broadly, "an oak was just a nut that stood its ground."

"Grandpa?" Annie spoke up, "Can you tell us a story about Great-grandpa Falcon?"

Falcon looked at Bill. "Just goes to show you the power of stories. She never tires of these. Okay Annie. But first let me tell Mr. West what Great-grandpa's job was," he looked over at Bill.

"My father was a wholesale gasoline dealer who sold to independent gas station owners. And let me tell you, those guys were tough customers. They were always trying to squeeze my Dad . . . even for a quarter-penny a gallon."

"Sounds familiar. My father imported and exported steel. He would lose deals . . . sometimes on less."

"Was your father successful at his business?"

"Very. He traveled all over the globe. Knew everyone."

"Well, Annie's Great-Grandpa Falcon loved the gasoline business, too. But do you think my father was successful because he had the lowest prices?"

Bill grinned, "I think I already know that answer."

"And you're right. Absolutely not! He was successful because he could tell great stories and he wasn't afraid to make real connections with people. He was lucky enough to live to meet our Annie here, though she doesn't really remember him. But he was pleased as punch to be a great-grandpa, and I try to keep him alive through stories I tell about him."

"They're my favorites," Annie grinned.

"OK. Let me see . . . I've got one . . . one weekend Great-grandpa Falcon was enjoying the 4th of July with me and my sisters and brothers. We were eating watermelon out on our front porch. And my gosh, it was one of the busiest weekends of the year. It was so good to see my Dad relax because that was when he told the best stories of all. I think he was telling us a story about this trip he once took to Alaska to go fishing for salmon. What a fish tale. He caught a salmon this big," Falcon stretched his arms wide.

"Well, lo and behold, here comes Mr. Parker. And he's walking pretty fast. He owned a gas station up the street from us. Apparently, Mr. Parker—who, by the way, wasn't a customer of my Dad's—had miscalculated how much gas he needed, because here he was on the busiest weekend of the year with a line of cars at his pumps and out of gas. He called everyone in town to try to get gasoline, but everyone said there was none to be had anywhere." The children leaned forward in anticipation.

"Did your Dad help him, Mr. Falcon?" Mike asked. "'cause my Dad hates it when people bother him on his day off."

"Well, Mr. Parker hated to bother my father when he was with his family. He knew how important my father thought family days were. But he stood to lose a *lot* of money. So he came up to my Dad, all red in the face, and told him of his predicament. And sure enough, my father told him a funny story from his own childhood about his mother miscalculating how much ice she was going to need, but she was a loyal customer of a great ice house so she was taken care of. See kids, back in those days, you kept food cold with big blocks of ice. So my Dad talked Mr. Parker into having some watermelon, while he got on the telephone and placed a couple of calls. And in less than 30 minutes, a whole truck-load of gas was delivered to Mr. Parker's gas station."

"Great-grandpa was a hero!"

"Sure he was. Everyone is the hero in his or her own story. They just have to believe that."

"Cute story," Bill smiled.

"More than cute, Bill. Powerful. Mr. Parker became one of my Dad's best customers, and my Dad must have told that story hundreds of times to new prospects. It was his most powerful sales tool. Why? Because information received at the emotional level is what influences people. A couple more things to remember about storytelling, Bill."

"Yes?"

"For one thing, always tell the truth. And be consistent. Remember that your stories have to match your behavior or you'll lose credibility. My father could tell the story about his mother forgetting the ice because that kind of unselfish humor matched who he really was."

"He sounds like a great guy."

"He was, Bill. I learned so much from him. Another thing I learned is to never try to make bad news sound good. If he didn't have any gas to give Mr. Parker, he wouldn't have tried to sugarcoat it. He would have been straight up with it. He was also a very good listener. And my three stars here know *all* about that, right?"

"Yes, Mr. Falcon. Listening is one half of the people equation."

"People equation?" Bill raised an eyebrow.

"Listening . . . sharing in return. Two sides of the same equation, Bill. Communicating is a contact sport. You make emotional contact with your audience. So stop telling and start sharing. Sharing creates intimacy, and intimacy creates relationships. And isn't that what you're trying to do after all— build lasting relationships? As an old Hasidic proverb says, 'Give people a fact or an idea and you enlighten their minds; tell them a story and you touch their souls.'"

As Falcon finished his proverb, a woman and a man approached the group, both in business suits.

"Hey Falcon, how was Mikey today?" said the man, obviously Mike's father.

"He's got some good news for you." Falcon grinned.

"Hey, that's right, Cowboy. Today was report card day," Mike's father bent down to hug his son.

"I did great!"

"I'm so proud of you," Mike's father picked his son up in

a bear hug. "Falcon, thanks. You know, I've been his biggest supporter this year. Rearranged my work schedule a bit. I just feel like all my priorities are falling into place."

"Harry, I'm telling you, supporting him now will pay off forever. Look at that proud grin." Falcon leaned over and mussed up Mike's hair. "See you at Saturday's soccer game, Champ."

"I'm gonna get a goal this week, I can feel it."

"Then you will, Mike. And no matter what, you'll be out there trying for the team."

"Bye Mr. West. Look . . ." Mike held up an acorn.

"What's that?"

"Arnie. A good luck charm. I'm going to keep him in my pocket at the game."

Bill winked at Mike. "Just remember . . . believe, Mike."

Jessica's mother came over to Falcon, "Hi Falcon. Thanks so much for spending the afternoon here with the kids. This means a lot to her. Soccer has become her favorite sport, and these Thursday afternoons . . . well, I just don't know how to thank you."

"You know, Janet, it's a two-way street. You're always so worried that this is an imposition. You're a wonderful mother who just so happens to be in the midst of accounting season. Don't worry. I get just as much out of my afternoons here."

"You know, Falcon, when you say that, I believe you. You've got a philosophy that makes a difference. See you Saturday?"

Falcon nodded and kissed little Jessica on the cheek. "Wouldn't miss our big game. Later, 'Gator."

After they were down the hill and out of sight, Bill turned to Annie and Falcon.

"You two hungry?"

Both nodded. "OK. My treat. Anywhere you want. What do you like to eat?"

"HAMBURGERS!" They both said, in perfect unison.

Annie laughed, "Personal jinx! Pinch, poke," she pinched and poked her grandfather, "you owe me a Coke. You're wearing black. You owe me a pack."

Falcon smiled ruefully, "I never remember to do that jinx thing. She beats me to the punch every single time!"

"Well . . . today that Coke's on me, too. Come on, you two. Let's go eat—somewhere where grass stains won't cause a scene."

The two men each took Annie by the hand and the three of them headed away from Arnie acorn and the great oak tree and into the fading sun. Bill turned back and stared at the oak and the fields where he'd acquired his grass and mud stains. He stuck his free hand into his pants pocket. He'd absent-mindedly put an acorn there. *This is more than just an afternoon of fun and games, Bill*, he said to himself. *Like the acorn, you just need to believe.*

BILL'S NOTEPAD

* Red Rover is over.

* Magic monster potion is created only by adding leadership that does not quash the child-like spirit.

* We must be consistent in all our stories; our stories must match our behavior.

* Kids communicate with no inhibitions. They speak from the heart. Strive to communicate person-to-person, heart-to-heart in everything we do.

* Stories create intimacy and relationships. And that's the essence of a strong brand.

* Have everyone share stories and listen to stories. Especially stories from our customers.

Chapter Eight

*To know even one life has breathed easier because
you have lived, this is to have succeeded.*

- Ralph Waldo Emerson

✳

They arrived at Falcon's and Annie's favorite hamburger restaurant named The King's. Elvis Presley glossy photos and memorabilia hung on every available inch of wall space. Elvis dolls and swivel-hipped singing knick-knacks adorned shelves. And of course, Elvis crooned out over the restaurant's sound system.

After following Falcon's recommendation and ordering two burgers with "the works," and a cheeseburger and chocolate shake for Annie, Bill leaned back against his side of the booth.

"You know Annie, your Grandpa's a pretty terrific guy, to watch your two soccer buddies on Thursdays—and to coach your team. I'm going to have to come to a game, now, you know."

"They're great kids." Falcon said as he winked at his granddaughter.

"Yeah," Bill agreed. " Mike's Dad seems like a nice guy. So does Jessica's Mom. They really admire you. I can see they appreciate what you do with those kids. I bet they never would have pictured a former CEO rolling up his sleeves and getting sweaty on the soccer field. Do you think Bill Gates will do that when he retires?"

"Maybe. But you know, Mike's Dad and Jessica's Mom have no idea I used to run a conglomerate."

"No? Do they know you from the garage then?"

"Nope. They know me as . . . Annie?"

"Coach, Sir!"

Both men laughed as little Annie mock-saluted her Grandpa.

"I think, Bill, that I'm very lucky—though to be honest, luck has little to do with it—in that people feel at ease around me. I purposely have worked to hone that skill. I want people to feel good about themselves when they're with me. I want the kids to feel good about themselves . . . and I want the parents to also."

"Well, then you've succeeded."

"Think about that word. 'Succeeded.' What does it mean to you?"

"I don't know. Earning the respect of my peers. Having the competition fear me. Taking the vacations I want. Going on safari. I don't know, really. What is it to you? Your garage full of classic cars?"

"It used to be. When I bought my first classic car, it was a thrill I can't describe. But since Annie became my teacher," Falcon reached lovingly around his granddaughter and pulled her closer to him, "I would have to say it's all about my brand. And my brand, what I want to be known for, is making others feel good about themselves."

"More like Emerson's view of success."

Falcon nodded. "To laugh often and much . . . to win . . . the affection of children."

"Blue Suede Shoes" came on over the sound system. "Now . . . that Elvis," Bill laughed. "*He* had brand."

Falcon nodded. "You may be kidding around Bill, but think about it. He really did. He was so popular, his brand of music made people feel so good inside, that they stayed with him through his drug abuse, obesity, and spandex jumpsuits. His brand endured even after he no longer exemplified it. Now, I'm not saying you should feel that you can abandon your brand personality and your customers will remain loyal, but I am saying that the connection is very emotional and it runs deep."

The waitress brought their drinks and a children's activity paper with crayons for Annie.

"Thank you, Ma'am," Annie smiled.

"Your welcome, young lady," the waitress smiled back.

"What have you got there, Annie?" Bill asked as Annie took her green crayon and began working on the puzzles and games on the paper.

"This puzzle." She showed Bill the classic nine-dot puzzle. "I have to use only four straight lines, and I can't lift up my crayon. And I have to connect *all* these dots."

"That's a tough one."

Annie nodded and bent her head in concentration.

"You know Bill, I've seen a consultant use this puzzle in a workshop. He talked about *mental* boxes and needing to think *outside* the box."

"Yeah. I've heard that before with a different prop."

"But you know, I'll challenge you one step further. It isn't about mental boxes."

"It isn't?" Bill looked puzzled.

"It's about physical boxes—our homes and our businesses. We go back and forth, back and forth, like rats in mazes. And sure, maybe we brainstorm here and there and try to think outside the box. Maybe we hire the best creative staff money can buy."

"Sounds familiar," Bill said, ruefully.

"Sure. You can come up with limitless ideas, but if you don't break out of your routine, if you don't connect to the bigger reality outside your physical box, all the creative ideas in the world won't help you. And what do you think is the most important puzzle to master?"

"Breaking routine?"

"To do what?" Falcon leaned forward. "Take it another level higher."

Bill shrugged. "Enlighten me, Falcon."

"The most important puzzle to master is understanding and communicating with your audience. Figuring out what people want and giving it to them. Helping them get the positive feelings they want, and eliminating the negative ones which they *don't* want."

"Falcon, again, it seems so *obvious*. I don't know . . ."

"But it isn't so obvious. What people think about *you* or your company is unimportant, Bill. What matters is how you make *them* feel about *themselves* and *their decisions* in your presence."

"The Falcon brand. Making them feel good about themselves."

"Sure. It's like falling in love. It's not about the other person as much as about how you feel when you're with them. How you're ten feet off the ground."

"It was twenty feet when I met my wife," Bill joked.

"Thirty when I met mine. It's like . . . hmm . . . have you heard the story about Benjamin Disraeli?"

"Nineteenth-century British Prime Minister?"

Falcon nodded. "Yes. The story I'm thinking of is about a young woman who dined one night with William Gladstone—another eminent statesman at the time. The next night, Disraeli accompanied her to dinner. And the woman later said, 'When I left the dining room after sitting next to Mr. Gladstone, I thought he was the most clever man in all of England. But after sitting next to Mr. Disraeli, I was sure that I was the most clever *woman* in England.'"

"Apparently she had a memorable encounter with Mr. Disraeli."

"Sure. The feelings he stirred in her about herself lingered long after the dinner was over. And that's your job, Bill, and the job of everyone in your organization. You have to enhance your customers' experiences with you each and every time they see you. And by you, I mean your people, your ads, your packaging, everything. That's the secret of capturing loyalty."

Annie looked up from her puzzle. "I did it!"

Both men looked at the paper and her green crayon marks.

"Watch. I'll do it again." With her crayon Annie drew four green lines and touched each of the nine dots without lifting the crayon.

"Good job, Annie," Falcon said. "You used your thinking cap. That's not an easy puzzle.

"Thank you, Grandpa." Annie beamed.

"Your Grandpa sure believes in you, Annie."

"Mm-hmm. He helped me learn this puzzle. And he tells me every day something good to believe about me. And now . . . it's gotten so I tell myself something good. That way, if anyone picks on me or says something not nice at school, then I just remember the good stuff and I don't feel so sad inside."

Bill looked at the two of them. "My guru and my teacher. You know, I'm starting to put this all together. If I can get each of my people to feel believed in and supported, then we can do anything as a company. It isn't about formulas. It's about heart-to-heart."

Falcon smiled. "A lesson well-learned, Bill."

Their dinners arrived and Bill felt himself overcome by hunger. "I sure worked up an appetite playing tag, Annie."

"Me, too!" She exclaimed as she grabbed a French fry and smothered it in catsup.

"So Falcon, when I leave you two tonight and I go back to the office, can it really be this simple? I mean, the marketplace is different from when you were at the top of your game. Advertising clutter, e-mail, faxes . . . how do I get my customers to listen to my brand. How does my company become, pardon the pun, 'The King'?"

"The marketplace is different?" Falcon asked.

"Sure," said Bill, biting into his burger.

"Wait just a minute." Falcon fumbled in his coveralls for a small black book. "I keep some of my favorite quotes in here. Are you ready?"

Bill nodded and Falcon read from the page he turned to. "Psychologists tell us the mind is under a continual bombardment of ideas, all of which are trying to make an impression upon it. The activities of a man's business that are going on about him, the people around him, the ideas that he has in mind to work out, the train of thought started by some object on which his vision rests—to say nothing of such commonplace things as his morning mail, his telephone and the papers on his desk—all claim his attention. And what is more, there is insistent demand that he attend immediately to one or several of these things. The prospect, therefore, does not sit around with his mind a blank, calmly waiting for someone or something to capture his attention without a struggle. The salesman enters a field already well occupied and must fight for the undivided attention that is essential to a successful sale. He must, by his personality, his proposition and by his opening remarks, eliminate all competitors for that attention and hold the field alone."

"You got it, Falcon. Exactly. I'm not telling you something you didn't already know. "

Falcon laughed. "Damn right I know it. The book this quote is from—*Modern Business*—was published in 1918. You see, Bill, getting someone's attention has *always* been a problem . . . and *always* will be."

"1918, huh? Okay then, how *do* you get their attention?"

"Well first let me tell you how *not* to do it. Forget about being loud or outrageous to be heard. Because only communication that connects will be listened to. Also, don't we all believe that the more we say, the more people will pay attention to us. It's simply not true. Rather, it's about relevance. Haven't you ever been at a party, involved in conversation, when all of a sudden you hear your name come up in another conversation? You were *hearing* the other conversation all along, but it wasn't until you heard your name —something that really matters to you—that you became aware of the other conversation."

"No handstands," Annie piped in.

"I beg your pardon?" Bill asked.

"No handstands, no grandstands. Grandpa likes people who don't tell you why they're so important. Everyone's important. Like Mr. Crenshaw."

"Mr. Crenshaw?"

"Dan Crenshaw is a fine old gentleman, about eighty-five years old. And he has a Studebaker that's his pride and joy. But he doesn't have a lot of money for repairs. And when he comes in, I make sure we take good care of his old car—just as much as we care for Bradley Hopper's cars."

"You take care of Brad Hopper's cars?"

"All thirty-seven of them. But I sometimes find the fact that he reminds me—every time he comes in—that he runs the number-one industrial chemical company in the world a little tiresome. That's not a story. That's a handstand."

As the trio finished their burgers, Bill pondered his leadership. Did everyone he come in contact with feel important? Did he make each and every contact count? Could the answer not be in the spreadsheets and instead be in empathy?

When they had finished, Bill grabbed the bill. "It's on me, don't forget."

"Time to get this little Missy home to bed," Falcon said as he slid out of the booth. "Mind if we stop there before the garage?"

"Not at all."

The three of them stood to leave. Bill looked down at Annie's tablemat.

"Can I have this, Annie? I like your doodles. And the way you solved your puzzle. I'd like to hang this on my wall at work."

Annie grinned. "Sure. I'll even draw you a picture of my dog Honey to give to you next time. I draw her really good 'cause I see her all the time, and I know every little thing about her."

Bill winked. "I'd like that." He picked up the tablemat. *Live outside the box. Break your routine. Connect the dots with empathy and compassion. The green crayon of an innocent child. A child not yet defined by rules, routines and narrow thinking.* Bill West smiled broadly. He could solve the puzzle now.

Bill's Notepad

* We must all live, as well as think outside the box if the company is going to succeed.

* It doesn't matter what people think about us. What matters is how we make them feel about themselves and their decisions in our presence.

* Connect the dots with compassion and empathy.

* Just as children respond to praise, so will my people.

* Gaining trust from the marketplace is more about connections than who can draw the most attention to themselves.

CHAPTER NINE

*The highest reward that God gives us
for good work is the ability
to do better work.*

- Elbert Hubbard

✳

On the ride home, Annie pulled a stuffed animal from her backpack and curled up with it in the back seat. Before they were on the road five minutes, she was sound asleep.

Bill turned around and looked at the sleeping child. In the pale light of the moon and highway lights, Annie's long lashes cast shadows on her cheeks. Her face was absolutely serene, like a photograph.

"You're a lucky guy, Falcon. She's beautiful, and she's certainly full of . . . I don't know . . . a love of people. The world hasn't battered her around yet. She has such enthusiasm."

"You know, we adults tend to feel the world is falling apart. And we want more intimacy because there's so much change in the world. So much we can't control. It just seems that children know how to grasp connections instantly. They have no artifice, and they aren't interested in holding you at arm's length."

"You know, Falcon, today seemed like such a long day to me. Not long in a bad way. It's just that when I'm at work, the day flies by, and all of a sudden I'm looking at my watch and it's 5:30. Today, it felt like it went in slow motion. We did so many different things, had fun with the kids . . . talked."

"I know what you mean."

"You want to know the scary thing?" Bill asked.

"What?"

"I feel like my life has flown by the last twenty years. Where the heck did it go? The time? You know, when I was in college, I would have called a guy my age 'old.'"

"If you're old then I'm ancient," Falcon laughed.

"Today just . . . I don't know . . . opened my mind about a few things."

"Bill, you want to know why life seems to pass so much slower when we're with kids . . . when we're *being* kids?"

"Yeah. Enlighten me. It was truly a strange feeling today."

"Okay. Well, when we're with children, and when we think like children—when we *were* children—every experience was fresh and new and exciting. So, you want your life to slow down? Then experience each day as the new. You know another thing about kids?"

"Hmm?"

Falcon gestured with his eyes to the back seat and whispered. "This is Annie's block. Watch how intuitive they are."

As soon as Falcon wheeled his Barracuda into Annie's driveway, the little girl stirred.

"Are we home, Grandpa?"

"Yes, Sweetie," Falcon said and winked at an amazed Bill.

"Don't you remember doing that when you were a kid?"

Bill smiled and nodded. "Guess you're right. I also remember thinking the moon was following me as my Dad drove us home at night."

The three of them piled out of the car and up the steps of a simple two-story Cape Cod home with a large picture window in the living room, where a dog sat staring at them, paws on the window sill.

Falcon pushed open the door. "My daughter's not home yet. Her car's not in the driveway. Because of this arrangement, Thursdays are good nights for Nina to work late, though she's usually home. I'm sure she'll be here any minute."

"Relax, Falcon. We'll just wait for her. Besides, I have to meet Annie's dog."

They both smiled as Annie knelt down, greeting her now-excited dog with an arms-around-the-neck hug. The golden-haired dog licked her face and danced, giving her the kind of greeting only a loyal dog can administer. Its entire body wriggled and wiggled, its yellow flag-like tail wagging from side to side.

"Mr. West, *this* is Honey. Isn't she wonderful?"

The animal lover in Bill responded. "She's lovely, Annie. And she sure loves you."

Annie nodded. "I've had her since I was a baby. We've grown up together."

Bill got on his knees to pet Honey. He looked up when they all heard Nina's keys jingling as she turned the doorknob and entered the house.

"Hi Dad. Sorry I'm late. I got caught up talking with three of my people as they picked up their kids from the daycare center."

"No problem, Bean." Falcon turned to Bill. "She hates it when I call her that. She's the CEO of a major technology company. But she's still Nina Beana to her old man."

Nina was bending down to kiss the top of Annie's head and offer a pat to Honey.

"Nina, this is Bill West," Falcon introduced them.

"Pleasure to meet you," Bill reached out to shake her hand. "I've spent the afternoon with your Dad and Annie. She's a fantastic kid."

Nina beamed. "Thanks." She put down her briefcase. "And I can tell by your suit, that you've been *playing* with my Dad. Again, I'm so sorry I was late. We have this onsite daycare center. I like to pop in there around 5:30 to say hello to the staff there and to see some of the kids off to their parents. It also gives my people a somewhat informal setting to talk to me. New people sometimes don't know what to make of the CEO sitting at those little kid tables in a little tiny chair, painting a watercolor or drawing with crayons. But then they get used to it and they like that I care enough about the center to make that part of my day, too. Listen, I hope I'm not holding you two up too much, but would you mind if I went and printed out an e-mail I need to send? I want my Dad's input before it goes out."

"Not at all," Bill said.

Nina disappeared upstairs as Bill, Falcon, and Annie went

to the kitchen to let Honey out the backdoor for a few minutes and to fill her food and water bowls. They returned to the living room as Nina came down the stairs.

"Here, Dad." She handed Falcon a printout. He started to read it over.

"Falcon?"

"Ya Bill?"

"I thought you were a big proponent of face-to-face. I wouldn't have guessed you'd be a fan of e-mail."

"I hope I didn't give you the impression today that I'm anti-technology, Bill. I certainly respect it. We just need to use it carefully. E-mail is simply another means to communicate, and I am all for communication."

"I try to use e-mail judiciously," Nina offered, as Falcon returned to reading. "I really believe in connecting to my people face-to-face. My people *are* my bottom line. Their knowledge, energy and loyalty are my most important assets. But I also need to stay connected as *often* as possible, and sometimes I just can't assemble my entire company together for a meeting. This helps me keep them involved. But I am also a big believer—thanks to the way my Dad raised me—of real human interaction. It's this human contact that drives my business. Gives us an edge."

"How's that, Nina? If you don't mind my asking."

"Watch out Bill." Falcon smiled. "She'll talk your ear off about that company of hers."

"Stop it Dad, you're embarrassing me," she laughed. She turned and winked at Bill. "But he's right. The key, Bill, is that my people interact more than any other company I am familiar with. In the halls. Over lunch. We have cookouts, education opportunities, brainstorming sessions. My people make frequent customer and supplier visits, and they make most of the decisions regarding our operation, not me. Every single person at my company is made to feel how valuable they are to the organization. You want to know something else?"

"Hmm?"

"Our turnover is virtually non-existent. And I have résumés pouring in from around the country. You see we've created a strong *employment* brand. Because what's a brand after all. It's about caring and culture, and a well-defined focused strategy. And more than anything, it's about trust. And heaven knows, it's a fragile bond. If we're all going to function in a stress-filled technology environment and enjoy it, I need to have them feel a bond to me *and* to the company's vision *and* to each other. If my people feel in control and appreciated, they'll become energized. Dad has always believed that networking these relationships—creating these feelings—is the major key to success."

"We talked about some of that today. How we're in the feelings business . . . identifying with people, and giving them what they want."

"He taught you the Falcon Rule, huh?"

"Do unto others exactly as they want done unto them." He gave Falcon a sidelong glance. "I'm a quick study. I just have to hope my people are. These are big changes in thinking."

"My father won't tell you all this . . . but he wasn't born with a silver spoon in his mouth by a long shot. He started at the bottom. A hard worker. So he had a clear focus on what a business ought to be."

"Take care of the customer." Bill said.

"Exactly. And then, as he started creating his own company, he knew he had to create a caring environment for the employees—Dad and I call them our associates—where they also want to focus on the customer. 'Do this, Bean, and there's no stopping you!'"

"He's right, I think. Especially after today. I certainly learned more today than in my MBA program."

Nina laughed, "Look how Dad's ignoring us. He's very modest. But you're right. He is a walking MBA program. He calls it 'Make Business *Audacious*.' Audacious meaning very bold or *daring*."

"But how did you create that kind of environment for your employees?"

"Well . . . I didn't want to wreck the culture itself—which already had great people in place willing to do anything for their company. So we took our time, let it develop, nudged it a little. Nurtured it. All the stuff Dad told you about, I'm sure."

Bill nodded.

Nina continued, "Well, the best part of it is that the philosophy he ingrained in me is now part of my employees' philosophies. It's more than a strategy. It's how we live. They all know there's nothing I wouldn't do for them. And because of that, there's nothing they won't do for me, or for each other."

Falcon looked up. "This e-mail is great, Bean. I especially like how you used flexibility in your word choices. A little vague."

"Vague is good?" Bill questioned.

"I think so," Falcon replied. "If you give people a little room to conjure up their own meanings, their own personal examples, the message itself becomes personal to them. Think about song lyrics. They let you think of your own first love, or first heartbreak. It's not so intensely personal that you can't relate."

"Sure," Bill said. "I can see that."

Nina interjected, "And it's the personal nature of the message that again makes them feel connected. Most of my employees have approached me at some point, and they all have the same story. They tell me at their old jobs, they felt lost, adrift. But in working for my company—for what they think of as 'their' company, now—they feel like they gained a community. A place where they can learn, collaborate and grow. They're part of my family, and they know that. They all have my home phone number. We care about and trust and respect each other. They're not human 'resources,' they're human beings. People with hearts and souls."

"Doesn't that drain you after a while?"

"Not at all. Think about how things were in the 'olden days,' as little Annie refers to them—of course she believes we're ancient," Nina smiled down at her daughter. "Families lived near each other. There was a sense of community and neighborhood. The word 'neighbor' actually meant something. Now, people can drive in and out of the same little gated community day after day and never really know another soul in their neighborhood. What I've done is create a real neighborhood at work. We've made a true paradigm shift. A new level of awareness. We relate to each other in a new way. We genuinely care for each other, and our customers, suppliers, and community. And we do this *while* rapidly adapting to all of this change we must go through."

Falcon looked at Annie sitting cross-legged on the floor, hands propping up her chin.

"We better get this little missy to bed."

All three adults accompanied Annie to her bedroom, decorated with her own artwork, pictures of Falcon and his wife, her friends, her dog . . . photos were everywhere. She had a poster of a dog on the wall, as well as one of John Donne's "No man is an island" phrase superimposed over a beach scene.

Annie went into the bathroom and brushed her teeth and put on her pajamas. As she returned to her bedroom, Falcon squeezed her and her mother to him at the same time. "These are my two beauties," he said. "And now this little angel must get some sleep."

Spontaneously, Annie ran over to Bill to hug him. "I had a great day today."

"Me, too, Annie. I hope we see each other again very soon."

Annie grabbed her stuffed animal and jumped into bed. Nina and Falcon both kissed her. Then Annie called out, "Honey!"

The dog bounded into the room, jumped on Annie's bed and curled down at the bottom.

"Goodnight everybody!"

"Goodnight, Annie," the adults called out, more or less in

unison. Nina turned off the bedroom light, and they descended the stairs.

"Bill, it was a pleasure meeting you," she said at the front door.

"Me, too."

She kissed Falcon. "I love you, Dad. Talking tonight just made me realize all the more how much of my philosophy I owe to you."

"You would have figured it out all on your own." He kissed her on her cheek.

Soon, the two men were back on the road, headed for Falcon's garage. When they arrived, Falcon asked, "Want to see my two other beauties?"

"Sure," Bill shrugged. Falcon parked the car, and they walked over to a garage in the back. When Falcon turned on the lights, Bill remarked, "This is a garage? It's so clean you could eat off the floor."

"Passion breeds care."

Falcon moved over to two cars and flicked on a second light so Bill could get a good look. Bill let out a long, slow whistle. "Wow!"

"Yup. This one's a '56 Chevy Belair Convertible."

"The two-tone red and white paint job is fantastic. What a car!" Bill said as he walked around the car, admiring the paint and the chrome.

"Now this one here," Falcon moved over to the second car,

a shiny white one, "is a 1953 Corvette. Only 300 were produced, and 200 were known to have survived. This baby is a real gem. I've been restoring her for longer than any other car I've worked on. The parts are nearly impossible to find."

"You're right. A beauty if I ever saw one. She's perfect."

Falcon moved around to the car's right front side. "Perfect. Except she's missing one hubcap here. Been looking everywhere for one. Calling in all my favors. No hubcap."

"Well, she's magnificent just the same."

"Thanks."

Falcon turned off the lights as the two men left the garage.

"I got a lot out of my day today, Falcon. I wasn't too sure when we started . . . God, that seems like it was days ago. But now . . . "

"Relationships are like mirrors Bill. You get out of them what you put into them."

"Well, I had a great one today, Falcon. You opened my eyes."

"All the answers to your problems were in your head all along, Bill. You just needed to tap into your heart to unlock them. Leadership is based on giving, not receiving."

"I can't thank you enough. And I would like to go to one of Annie's soccer games. Mind if I call you to set it up?"

"Bill, we're friends now. Call anytime."

They shook hands, and Falcon slapped Bill on the back. Bill climbed into his car and waved good-bye as he drove away.

Bill West mulled over the day again and again, smiling at key points as he reflected on the lessons he learned. He drove across town to his home and pulled into his driveway. He knew his wife would be at her weekly book group, so the house was dark, and he fumbled for his keys at the door.

Entering his house, his menagerie of pets greeted him and he fed, walked and watered the cat and his dogs. He fed the fish and his birds; it was always his way to unwind after a busy day. Then he went upstairs to take off his grass-stained clothes and to shower.

In his bedroom, he picked up his portable phone as he flicked on the light. It was habit. He dialed his voice mail.

The electronic voice spoke, "You have . . .15 new messages."

"Damn," he sighed, and started listening to them.

"Bill, this is Ray. Croton and Sons reneged on the deal. We need to talk about a counter-offer. This is a colossal pain in the ass. I don't need to tell you how many hours I put into this . . ." Beep.

"Bill? Karen. Listen, I need to know what you want me to do about the Morris account. He insists if we don't do better on price this year he is going to drop us. But we've kept him at the same price for three years now. I vote for letting him go. Where else is he going to get a deal like ours?" Beep.

Bill West felt himself fall naturally into "CEO"-mode. He pressed 8 on his phone to respond to Karen, his back muscles tightening.

"Karen, Bill here. Listen, I think we need to have a sit-down with Morris. I don't like that he keeps holding our feet to the fire. Talk to me first thing tomorrow. Friday."

He listened to the next voice mail.

"Bill. Randy Black here. Listen, I get the impression that your sales manager thinks he can screw around with what has been a long-standing agreement between us. This is a bunch of crap and you know it." Beep.

"Bill, this is Marv . . ."

Bill continued listening to his voice mail, growing tenser by the moment, as he walked over to his dresser. He kept an old cigar box on his dresser that belonged to his grandfather. He opened it with one hand as he started emptying his change and receipts into the box. Quarters, nickels, and dimes clinked against the existing change. He was still listening intently to his messages when an acorn landed on the change.

"Arnie," he whispered. Suddenly, the voice mail seemed a thousand miles away. He clicked off the phone and placed it on his dresser. A rush of shock filled him. How could he have forgotten everything so quickly, slipped back into the old mind-set? The old way of doing things? He picked up the acorn and stared at it.

"If we're going to be mighty, I need to live each day like today . . . at the park. Playing tag." He was aware he was whispering to himself. "The genius of childhood, Arnie, my friend. The genius of childhood."

Shaken by how tense he had allowed himself to get, Bill went over to his bed and sat down. The house seemed very still, and he could hear his own breathing. He didn't know how long he sat there reflecting on his life when he heard his wife come into the house.

"Bill?" she called.

"Up here, Angel."

He sat on the bed, waiting for her to make her way up the stairs.

"You're just getting home?" she asked, noting he was still half-dressed in his suit.

"Yeah, Hon. Sit down. I've had the most amazing day. "

She sat beside him, and he grasped her hand.

"I have so much to tell you," he said softly, as he began. "It all started when I met this guy Falcon at a gas station . . . ."

BILL'S NOTEPAD

* Experience each day as new and fresh.

* Our company must feel like a neighborhood to its employees.

* Our people are our bottom line.

* Respect technology, but use it carefully.

* I must give, not receive, if I expect to be a great leader to my associates.

* If people feel in control and appreciated, they'll become energized.

* We crave intimacy in this fast-paced world where everything seems out of control.

CHAPTER TEN

I must go now, for there go my people,
and I am their leader.

- Gandhi

✳

Falcon steered his white Corvette through the summer sun, the brilliant sheen of the well-polished car bouncing the rays of the sun off its hood and literally gleaming. He didn't drive the Corvette often, but today was a special day. The car was perfect, except for the missing hubcap; she was the best restoration he had ever done.

Glancing to his right, Falcon saw that Annie was engrossed in a book.

"What are you reading, Annie?"

"A biography of Helen Keller, Grandpa."

"But it's summer," he teased. "Why are you reading *books*?"

"Books are the key to knowledge, Grandpa. Books and experience. You know that."

"Do I?"

Annie laughed, her smile revealing two newly grown front teeth. "Yes! You're the one who told me that. Stop being so silly."

Falcon grinned. Annie always said what was on her mind.

He looked up at a highway sign. According to the directions, he had four more exits to go. As he drove, he noticed people speeding up to catch a closer glimpse of the Corvette, and he smiled to himself. Finally, he reached their exit and made a right-hand turn. On the corner was the church Bill told him about. The pastor was nearly as fond as Falcon of sayings, and he displayed them on a sign in the church's front yard. "Faith is caught, not taught."

"Ain't that the truth," Falcon whispered to himself.

"Ain't isn't a real word, Grandpa."

"Sorry Sweetie. I didn't even realize I spoke out loud."

He drove down a short stretch of road and into an industrial park. He found the building.

"Come on, Annie," he said as he parked the car and helped his granddaughter scramble out.

Walking through the front entrance of Bill's company, Falcon sensed an electricity in the air. The first thing he noticed was the chatter. As employees walked through the lobby on their way to meetings or other parts of the building, they walked in clusters, clearly engrossed in their conversations. And what he heard in snatches of expressions wasn't gossip. "The customer wants it, so let's make sure we . . ." "Bill gave our team the go-ahead on this new idea . . . "

As the employees walked by, Falcon also noticed something else. Smiling. Joking. He overheard one exchange in which the two people disagreed with each other, but they each listened to the other. Falcon nodded his head in silent approval.

"Can I help you, Sir?" An older man stopped and smiled at Falcon and Annie. "Our receptionist is out today. Her daughter, Katie, is in a play this afternoon and we're very liberal here about time off for family. She's playing Dorothy in the Wizard of OZ."

"You sound like her agent," Falcon joked.

"No . . . but that's something about our company. We're not nosy, but we do all know about each other's families and kids and lives. In a caring way. I'm not sure why . . . it sort of happened over the last six months or so. Anyway," he kneeled down to shake Annie's hand and look her in the eye, "how can I help you two?"

Falcon spoke, "I'm Richard Falcon, and this here is Annie Cortez, my granddaughter."

"This is Miss Annie Bananie?"

Annie giggled and nodded. The man lifted her up and gave her a little spin, placing her back down again.

"Well, I'll be . . . and Falcon. *The* Falcon. Let me shake your hand. I'm John Stasinos. And it is truly a pleasure to meet you. Bill told us you were coming. You know, after he met with you, he came back and told us a story. In fact, he told us many stories, but he told us one important one about a day he spent with you and Annie here. He told us fear would no longer be our motivator. We would build a revitalized company based on caring and trust. He wouldn't tell us to follow him. Instead, he would come to us for the direction. No roadmap, just the essence of true leadership and," John hesitated for a moment.

"Go on," Falcon smiled.

"Well, he was patient . . . a believer in *us*. We weren't employees anymore. We were part of the solution. He said he would never give up and he wouldn't let us fail."

"Sounds like a powerful meeting."

"It was," John looked Falcon in the eyes. "A few people were wiping their eyes. Bill was very emotional too. Before that meeting with you, we all thought maybe we'd be looking for new jobs soon. That he'd sell the company. But after that . . . " John shook his head, the memory clearly a strong one. "Well, put it this way, I feel like six months ago I did get a new job at a new company—only I never left this one. And look at the wall over there."

"The spot where the paint's a different color?" Annie asked.

"Yeah. That's where we used to have a sign. A mission statement. Only it really didn't mean much to us. To any of us. It was just a fancy-sounding paragraph. So Bill took it down. But he asked us not to repaint over the spot, made us keep it looking different. So that when we came in every day, we would remember . . . how did he put it? That we are more than a mission statement. We are living a mission." John Stasinos paused. "Oh look." He smiled broadly and gestured with his hand as if he were introducing a celebrity. "Here comes Mom."

Falcon turned as an elegant young woman approached them.

"Mom?" he asked, as he extended his hand.

She laughed. "Just a joke. My name is Deanna Cunningham. Bill hired me about 6 months ago to help revitalize the products division. Gave me a unique title in a company where titles aren't so important anymore. But mine is Manager of Mentoring."

"M.O.M. I get it," Falcon smiled.

"And I heard all about you and Annie here. I even heard about your bird . . . about Honey, your dog. About many things, Annie. Bill gave me notes he took that day. More importantly, we went out for dinner and he told me the story of the whole day. It was then that I knew I'd take the job. Here he comes."

Falcon and Annie turned and Annie darted off in a spontaneous run. Bill lifted her up and gave her a big bear hug, carrying her back to Falcon, John, and Deanna.

"Is your hair faintly pink, Bill?" Falcon laughed as the two men shook hands.

"Lost a bet with my entire marketing department. This is very faded. You should have seen it Wednesday."

"I can attest," John was laughing out loud. "He looked like a refugee from a punk rock band."

"Annie?"

"Yes, Mr. West?"

"Do you want to go with Deanna and John here? Today is Freaky Friday in the lunchroom. All the employees bring their kids to eat with them, and we have entertainment. I think today is a magician and a clown. And we have a special menu in the cafeteria. Hot dogs . . . chicken nuggets. Macaroni and cheese. Ice cream. Make your own sundae. I bet, because I knew you were coming, there's even some peppermint stick."

"You remembered!"

"Would never forget, Annie."

"Can I go, Grandpa?"

"Sure, Sweetie. See you later."

John and Deanna each took her by the hand and led her off.

"I didn't know what to expect Bill. But I sense it. The place is alive."

"Thanks Falcon. It certainly hasn't been easy.

"Helping people change the way they think never is, Bill."

"And 'Mom', Falcon? She's wonderful. Ph.D. in psychology. She just understands people."

"Exactly what any company needs."

"Well, I started thinking, I had all these B-school people. Great people with great ideas. But we needed some balance. We needed the people side. We lost it—or maybe we never had it. Anyway, care for the nickel tour?"

The two men went from department to department. Everywhere Falcon was impressed by the palpable excitement in the air.

"And here," Bill said as they opened the door to another department. "I am most proud of this."

They walked down a short corridor and entered a large room where a variety of people sat around a huge conference table. Pizza boxes and soda cans were at one end, and seated around the table, employees were drawing with crayons, cutting out designs from cardboard. The group was an eclectic mix—old and young, Generation X'ers . . . a couple of high school age kids.

"Interns?" Falcon asked, spying them.

"Yup."

The group had smiled as the two men entered, but they continued their debates. The conversations were both playful and provocative, friendly, yet they were clearly unafraid to speak their minds.

"When I came back from our meeting, I thought a lot about branding," Bill whispered so as not to disturb the team. "So I gathered this team together, and we talked about the feelings business."

"I wonder where you ever got that crazy idea," Falcon winked.

"Have no idea," Bill playfully replied. "But we talked about feelings nonetheless. And everyone kept coming back to design. From marketing to Web site design to product design . . . we decided no more functionality without beauty. Aesthetics are important. It equals feelings. So we made a connection between our designs and excited, happy customers."

"And a brand was born."

"You got it."

"This team here," Bill gestured to the table, "they take their work very seriously, but not themselves. Work should be fun. Can you believe I'm saying that? Can you believe I know that . . . I believe it with all my soul. My people, their sense of fun, this branding . . . we're achieving results we've never experienced before. Out of sight."

"That's the essence of uncovering the intuitive."

"Right," Bill opened the door so they could move on. "Our customers want things faster. They want it NOW. They want it customized. They want convenience. They want to be catered to. We used to spend most of our time looking for customers for our products. Now, we're out searching for products—and solutions—for our customers. And my people sense this intuitively. They're moving toward the realm of unconscious competency."

"Now that's a new one to me."

"Deanna explained it to me. See, there's unconscious incompetence. You don't even know what you don't know."

"OK. I got you," Falcon nodded.

"Then there's conscious incompetence. You're aware of what you don't know. And there's conscious competence. You know what you know."

"Like I know you look ridiculous with pink hair?"

Bill gave Falcon a sidelong glance. "Yeah, wiseguy. Sort of like that. And then there's unconscious competence. Like artists. You don't even know what you know. You can just do it. It's part of you."

"I hear you. I'm going to remember that one."

The two men walked down a hall toward the cafeteria.

"This has been the hardest six months of my life. But the most rewarding. My employees are my friends . . . my family. I feel excited again. Passionate . . . the way your daughter is. And watching them—us—grow and learn and excel . . . it's a joy."

"Isn't it though? You've got radical honesty going on here. People not afraid to approach you, not afraid to make mistakes."

"Like my hair. Not afraid to get muddy . . . or look foolish. It's about giving up the compulsion to control everything. Freedom from the grind. The e-mails I can let go of. The voice mails someone else can handle. The nonessential stuff can wait. The people and feelings can't."

The two men entered the cafeteria where it appeared most of the company had gathered. Annie ran over to Falcon.

"Grandpa . . . they have a cake! For us. For me and you!!"

She led him by the hand to a table where a cake sat. It was white, and on the top was an elaborate icing picture. It was a sandbox with a red bucket in it. Across the top of the sheet cake were the words, "Sandbox wisdom will release your inner child." Across the bottom of the cake was "To Annie and Falcon with Love!!"

Falcon was deeply touched. He squeezed Annie's hand and pulled her close to him. She had the wisdom. He had merely learned to absorb it instead of being caught up, as Bill had once been, in all of the day-to-day minutiae.

"Everyone," Bill shouted, as he climbed atop a chair, "I want to gather you all together. Come on over here."

The employees gathered around the cake table. Excitement rippled through the crowd.

"As you all know, we owe a debt of gratitude to Falcon and Annie here. I personally do, and you all know how we've all changed thanks to the lessons and insights I learned from them. I know Falcon. He wouldn't like the words 'debt of gratitude.'"

Falcon nodded in agreement.

"So I merely want to say, 'Thank you friends.' And I would like you to have these gifts."

Bill handed Annie a wrapped present. She quickly tore it open. "A book!"

"Arnie the Acorn," Falcon whispered and ran his finger across the title. "Marcy West?"

"My wife. She always wanted to write a book and illustrate it. I just encouraged her to follow her dream. We self-published it. Can't keep enough in print."

"Thank you," Annie clutched the book to her chest.

"And Falcon . . ." Bill handed him a package. Falcon tore open the paper, as all the employees leaned forward in anticipation. Inside the box was a shiny hubcap.

"Oh my . . . " Falcon felt himself choke up. He looked up, "How did you . . . ?"

"I didn't do anything."

A chorus of voices in the room said, "We did!"

Bill explained. "I couldn't find it Falcon, so I turned it over to the most dedicated team I know. All of them. They found it. I am totally convinced. They can do anything. Plus . . ." Bill added with a smile. "No one is as smart as everyone."

"Thank you," Falcon said genuinely moved. "I'm grateful I could be some small part of this energy."

"Come on," Bill said, "Let's cut this cake."

After cake and coffee, it was time for Falcon and Annie to go. Bill walked them to the front door.

"Stay true to your wisdom, Bill."

"I will, Falcon."

He bent down to hug Annie. "And you . . . you stay true to all you feel inside, Annie."

"I will, Mr. West." She kissed his cheek.

Annie and Falcon left the building and walked to the Corvette. Falcon opened his trunk and pulled out a tool, placing the hubcap on the bare wheel. He stood up and stepped back.

"What do you think, Annie?"

"It's beautiful!"

Falcon tousled her hair. "Let me get you home."

The two of them drove away. Falcon looked in his rearview mirror. "Look behind us Annie."

She turned around. A couple of dozen employees were waving as they left the parking lot. Annie waved furiously until they were out of sight. Soon, they were on the open highway, the Corvette gleaming in the setting sun.

"Grandpa?"

"Yeah, Love bug?"

"That day? That day with the sandbox and the bird, and the ice cream and all?"

"Yeah . . ."

"Did it really help Mr. West that much? I mean, he gave me this book and everything."

"Yes Sweetie. But here's a secret. All those changes he made to his company? They were inside him all the time. He just sort of forgot. See, grownups get big and they forget all the things they know about people and love and feelings. It just gets lost in all the seriousness of being a grownup."

"Do grownups have to be so serious?"

"No, Sweetie, they don't. Not at all."

"Does everybody have those things inside them?"

"Yes, Annie they do. They just forget. Luckily, I have you, so I can't ever forget."

Richard Falcon drove down the highway toward the setting sun. He glanced over at Annie. He had his hubcap. He had feelings in his life. He had sandbox wisdom and, most importantly, he would never let it go.

BILL'S NOTEPAD

* It's all about faith . . . and love.

CLOSING THOUGHTS

*The secret of genius is to carry the spirit
of the child into old age.*

- Aldous Huxley

✵

*F*am acutely aware that it was your *choice* to read this
book, so thank you very much for taking the time and
allowing me to share my thoughts with you. I truly appreciate
it. And I hope that through this simple fable, you have
rediscovered the "truth" about business and are inspired to do
something special with *your* business—and with your life.

I'd love to hear your thoughts about *Sandbox Wisdom*. I'm
also available if you have any questions or if you'd like to
bring the power of *Sandbox Wisdom* to your organization in
the form of a keynote speech, or a custom presentation or
workshop. You can reach me directly via email by visiting
www.sandboxwisdom.com.

Ray Bradbury wrote that "If we listened to our intellect,
we'd never have a love affair. We'd never have a friendship.
We'd never go into business, because we'd be cynical. Well,
that's nonsense. You've got to jump off cliffs all the time and
build your wings on the way down." Your dreams and
aspirations are important. They're what give life meaning.
So keep your dreams and never waiver in your faith. Take
risks and be a loving, playful, passionate human being.